Endorsements

"Harrison Meagher has written a powerful guide to healing every part of ourselves. He has broken the chains of conformity to write this book – giving it a rhythmic cadence that is trance inducing, spiritual, healing and all at once useful. The practicality of his exercises and the heart of his prose make this a book I will read time and time again. Follow his bountiful wisdom and courageous journey of healing while he invites you into your own. If you let it, this book will crack your heart open!"

– **Claudia de Llano, Marriage and Family Therapist,** Author of *The Seven Destinies of Love*

"Harrison Meagher's book is like a long, cool drink of water for the spirit who has endured many sweltering days. He explains concepts that have been previously confusing in a way that is simple, clear, and most importantly, memorable. For example, our previous misunderstanding of karma is laid to rest; and the reader is able to walk away with an understanding of karma as balanced or unbalanced energy and choices. I found Harrison's writing to be soothing to body, mind, spirit, and soul. He is definitely the kind of loving guide I want walking with me on my journey from head to heart. This book belongs in the hands of anyone who is committed to understanding their soul's journey on a deeper level and enhancing their sacred love frequency."

– Stephanie Banks, highly sought-after Intuitive Channel, Author and Speaker

"This book is a powerfully reverent chronicle of a journey on the path to freedom, in which Harrison Meagher generously and skillfully shares wisdom to support us on our own. Precision. Grace. Compassion. LOVE. These a few of the sacred gifts you'll receive from these pages."

– Michelle Veneziano, Family Medicine Physician, Intuitive, Author and Educator

"If you are on a path to discover your unique gifts this is a must read! What if we were to look at the world through the Lens of Love? How would this paint the landscape of your life? Harrison weaves a masterpiece of guided information on how to look at life through this lens of Love. I have watched Harrison live by the example of all that he has written. I have had the honour to watch his transformation. His growth is inspirational, his work is effective and his approach is organized. As I read this book I connected with my own Cosmic Love Antenna; the desire I have had in me welled up once again. What is my channeled message? Upon sharing this with Harrison he affirmed that this was his intention! That those who read this book open up to their gifts & unique love frequency."

– Claudia Moriel, Frequency Medicine Practitioner, Biohacker and Educator

"Harrison lovingly guides your soul to explore its deepest shadows while experiencing its highest light. Every concept is meant to be healing to your soul, therapeutic to the mind and nourishing to your body. This is your cosmic map to travel back to the heart."

– Dr Taggy Bensaid, Naturopathic Doctor & Soul Surgeon

"Harrison Meagher is one of the most gifted and effective healers I have ever met. He has the ability to tap into spiritual energies and cut through the noise to get to the heart of the matter in any healing journey. This book distills much of his wisdom in a beautiful, free and poetic format. It is a must read for any healer or anyone on a quest to become their higher self."

– Emi Hosoda, Board Certified Internal,
Functional & Holistic Medicine MD

Your Cosmic Love Antenna

Your Cosmic Love Antenna

*Define, Embody & Emit Your
Unique Frequency of LOVE*

By

Harrison Meagher

© 2023 by Harrison Meagher

All rights reserved. This book or any portion thereof may not be reproduced or used in any manner whatsoever without the express written permission of the publisher except for the use of brief quotations in a book review.

ISBN: 978-0-6457065-0-5 | 978-0-6457065-1-2 (E-BOOK)

*Disclaimer:

This book is not intended to be a substitute for the medical advice of a licensed physician.

The reader should consult with their doctor in any matters relating to his/her health.

Dedication

To my Mother who planted the love seed,

my Father for giving me the tools to help it grow

and all of the individual souls who have inspired and reflected the courageous sunshine needed to share my love frequency with the world.

Table of Contents

Author's Note	xii
Acknowledgments	xiii
Introduction	xiv
Part 1: Mind	1
1 Holding the Inner Child	3
2 The Ancestral Breaker of Chains	23
3 The Healthy Ego	38
Part 2: Body	61
4 The 3D Tells a Story	63
5 Your Physical Pillar	79
6 Chakra Gateways	98
Part 3: Soul	111
7 The Longest Road of All	113
8 Heart-Space Portal	130
9 Your Loving Divinity	151
Conclusion	172
Resources	176

Author's Note

This book breaks all the rules of grammar, punctuation and writing in its traditional format.

This book is a conversation, song, poetry, prose and a stream of conscious love frequency intended to be conveyed as it was received.

Please pause in moments, take your time and soak up that which is in the spaces between words.

Enjoy the journey.

With love,

Harrison Meagher.

Acknowledgments

Taylor Meagher – My beautiful & divine sister who has produced and channeled the cover art piece for this publication. More information on her work and offerings can be found at www.taylormeagher.com

Claudia de Llano – My dear friend, colleague and cheerleader who has inspired and compassionately pushed me along every step of this book production journey. Without her insight and love I am positive this gift would not be here in your hands in its current form. More information on the love she is channeling into this world can be found at www.theawakenedjourney.com

All of you reading these words right now. Thank you for allowing your heart to guide you to this expression of my love.

Introduction

We live in a world where the mind and the thinking, logical ego have supremacy.

I say this without judgment or ill will.

I say this as an observation about what is needed, and what is needed is more time spent in our hearts.

What is needed is more time in our love,

what is needed, and I want to say this for all to feel,

is a deeper understanding of what it means to show up, whether it is with our family or friends, in our work, or with our passions or purpose,

to show up in our love frequency rather than through our minds or unhealed egos.

If we can do this, we will be interacting with reality through our lens of love and moving beyond limitation and separation.

Twenty-Four Years Ago...

As I sat on my bed noticing and feeling the energy and sensations moving through my little body, there was a rush of excitement but also fear.

When I think back on that young boy, who is very much still in me, here, as I share these words with you, I wonder and question if he anticipated what would come.

Both the negative and the positive.

I was connected to my body in a new way.

I started to feel and understand new sensations and new functions of my being, which mostly originated down in my sexual organs,

I must have been no more than seven or eight, but again, reflecting back in this moment, those feelings were viewed as very mature, and I was reminded of this oddity over the next few years.

Based on my environment in the school system I was in, my parents (despite there being so much love flowing between us),

who also came into this world with their own set of belief systems, trauma, and pain,

I pushed away that little boy who was excited and was experiencing the full spectrum of all of this.

I pushed away that little boy who was discovering himself at that point in time in new, sexual, sensual, and loving ways.

A big reason for this was fear.

What if others didn't like me and rejected me?

What if I was different?

What if I was pushed away and left alone?

The little boy that was instilled inside of me as Harrison was punished, suppressed, and eventually numbed.

Not only the sexual and sensual feelings moving in him but also his sensitivities, emotions, and spirit overall.

I can point to many events in which this was incubated, but the larger image and theme I aim to express as we go deeper into this book and journey ahead together

is that this early-childhood experience of suppression and ignoring big parts of my being

fundamentally impacted my relationship to love.

It fundamentally impacted my understanding of what love actually is.

I grew up in a world that taught me to be a man who was strong but quiet.

I grew up in a world that taught me not only that the sensitive, vulnerable, and emotional side of my being was not connected to love

but also that it detracted from my power.

And that very power also lay outside of me.

I add that last component because I grew up in a religious environment.

I wouldn't say my parents were particularly religious, but I went to a religious school and was raised in a religious culture overall,

which taught me and displayed to me that this power I was seeking to balance through the suppression of my emotional sensitivities and sensuality was outside of me, on a cloud, keeping score.

Judging.

So this led to more disconnection, again, from what love actually meant to me.

So, in my adolescence—because love, I've now come to see, is so fundamental and intrinsic to my beingness—

I unconsciously looked for an understanding and more answers to this love question in the external world, be it in superficial sexual relationships

or in losing myself in alcohol, drugs, and the highs of travel and adventure.

All of these had the fundamental underpinning of seeking something, of seeking love externally while also pushing away any inklings that this love could be connected to my power.

That this love could be connected to more than the individual of who I was.

Fast-forward a few more years and this externalization of myself,

this externalization of my love, has led to an inevitable, deeply painful breaking point.

The force of love inside of me—which was longing to be felt, longing to be acknowledged, longing to be expressed through my being.

It had to get my attention somehow, and due to my inability to go within, my inability to look and feel inside, it had to get my attention in the outside world.

How did it do this?

It did this by instantly taking away everything I had defined as *me* through a fearful, scary, and traumatizing experience of being detained, jailed, and deported.

I was left with only myself, and it was here, by myself, in myself, and through myself, that I had to do things a little bit differently.

I had to get back to that little boy, who was still inside of me.

That little boy who wanted to feel,

who wanted to express,

who wanted to acknowledge the excitement for all that he was

but wanted to do it in a way that was wholesome.

A way that didn't ignore parts of himself—a way that acknowledged not just his inner masculine and feminine but how that energy was expressed through his mind, his body, and his spirit,

and this is the journey that I want to take you on now.

It's not just a journey of synchronizing your mind, body, and spirit but also a journey of the beautiful emotions that link these three parts of our being together.

That bridge these parts of our being.

But what happens when we achieve synchronization?

When we achieve synchronization, something very powerful occurs, something I call the activation of your cosmic love antenna.

This is the love frequency, the love energy, the love essence that is not only what you are but what you came to express in the world.

This love frequency holds not just your healing,

not just your deeper layers of transformation across that mind-body-and-spirit spectrum

but also all of the light and gifts and passion you deserve to express in this 3D world, during one's time here.

So come on this journey with me today.

Join me and little Harrison, and let's switch on your cosmic love antenna.

―――

With that in your heart, let's answer the question you probably have: What is your cosmic love antenna?

Put very simply, it is what you are.

You are a beautiful, abundant, and loving antenna of mystical, spiritual love.

Much like an antenna system, you have two main components.

You have the outside shell or casing that allows the internal energy or frequency to be emitted out into the universe.

And then, of course, as just outlined, you have the internal frequency. That internal frequency is your love frequency, and the external structure is made up of your mind, body, and spirit.

So, to become a cosmic love antenna and start embodying, defining, and expressing your love frequency, you must harmonize and synchronize your mind, body, and spirit so that your love frequency can flow,

because at the end of the day, this is not about gaining your love frequency.

This is about pulling back the layers stopping the expression and sharing the answer that's been there the whole time.

Whether it's through our mental gardens, our physical rejuvenation, or our connection to our soul/spirit, we must come together to allow the frequency to be expressed so our cosmic love antenna will be strong.

Now let's take an additional moment to explain what, exactly, your love frequency is.

How many times have you asked yourself why you are here?

How many times have you wondered what your unique gifts are?

How many times have you asked the mirror what the point is?

Your love frequency answers these questions.

Your love frequency is the blueprint of your soul.

Your love frequency is how your unique soul expression stands in its power within this 3D form and world.

Your love frequency is what gives you that beautiful, powerful uniqueness in all your glory.

When you start to find, define, and emit your love frequency, you are being all of yourself in any given moment,

and while these *selves* are constantly changing and evolving throughout your journey, you can come back to this unique frequency consistently.

Another way to describe this is *authenticity*.

This is you showing up in all of your divine beauty.

Your love frequency might move through you in one of your gifts, whether this be through your *clair* senses, your clairvoyance, clairaudience, your clairsentience (spiritual senses),

whether this be through your ability to channel,

whether this be through the written word, the spoken voice, or the physical movement,

all of these are external layers in which your love frequency is shared with the world.

So, put simply:

your love frequency is you in all of your uniqueness, and the more you can get familiar with it, the more you can show up in the spaces and places you wish in your fullest expression.

Let us add another definition to your love frequency, just to be safe.

Your internal space and then, ultimately, your external expression of love, is another ripple and characteristic of the unique soul expression that you are.

How much you can define and embody and ultimately express your love frequency

is also the extent to which you can express the unique soul that you are within this world.

So, as we go further and deeper, keep this in the back of your mind and in the back of your heart,

understanding that the more love you emit, the more your soul and spirit are expressing their unique frequency to all of those who need it, including yourself.

As we take a journey together in this book and move through the different chapters, I want you to see this experience firstly as a cosmic dance.

On my podcast, *The Cosmic Love Antenna*, when I have an interview or I'm doing a solo episode, sharing from my heart to hit yours,

I set the parameters to have a cosmic dance with myself and you, the listener,

and what I mean by this is that our energies come together to cocreate something more,

and what I wish for this book to give you today is for us to dance through these words and through the frequency that I share behind them.

If you can see this as a loving dance, then you can receive the channels, the wisdom, the guidance that goes so much deeper than the letters on the page.

—— ——

The final grounding element that I want to share with you as we start this experience together is that I would ask you to set an intention for what you wish to get out of this reading.

Remember that when you set an intention around anything, especially a mystical, spiritual experience,

much like what you will get out of this book, you open and channel your potential and set it down a specific path or direction.

Remember, what is an intention?

It is your beautiful inner power in resistance or friction with something else.

So you channel this potential into a direction that you deserve to have manifested.

So I would ask you to place your hands on your heart.

Drop into that mystical heart space, even if this is new to you, and set an intention for these words ahead.

It could be as simple as experiencing your love frequency or feeling love or understanding what love looks like inside of you.

Set this intention. Remove all expectations. And let's go on a journey together into your deep depths of love.

Before stepping into the garden of your mind along our path, let us take some time now and first talk about the synchronization of mind, body and soul overall.

Something you will hear me speak about a lot throughout this book and the experience that you will have with me is

that this is not about adding on but rather pulling back a truth that has been in you this whole time.

And this truth is that you are a beautiful system of systems that dynamically move together throughout time and space with loving intention.

What I mean by this is that this beautiful system of systems is what makes you up across mind, body, spirit, and the emotional bridge.

This system is holistic, and in being holistic, you are more than the sum of your parts.

You are more than just a physical being.

You are more than just a mental being.

You are more than just a spiritual being.

You are all three plus the emotions that connect them all together.

So if we're looking to start to enhance and amplify and embody our love frequency, we must approach our body with a synchronistic approach and lens.

That's really the first understanding I want to help you see, and I will break down mind, body, and spirit in the chapters ahead.

What I want to do in this introduction is really to talk about the glue that ties them all together.

And this glue is your emotions.

Your emotions, put very simply, from my experience, are energy in motion.

You are energy at a very fundamental state.

Everything on and around you is in an energetic field that is connected within this divine, eternal, present moment.

Through the quantum lens, the future and the past are warping into the current moment, so,

all of those fancy words aside, what I'm helping you see here is that the more emotional and, more specifically, the more *energy in motion* we can be, the more *us* we can be.

This is something that is thrown around a lot in spiritual, mental, and emotional communities.

But I want to take you a little bit deeper here and explain why this is important.

While through a spiritual lens, I truly acknowledge the fact that we are *not* our emotions,

through my lens you're actually the container of love or, more specifically, the cosmic love antenna that holds the emotions,

but what the emotions and what this *energy in motion* are

is a powerful communication device.

But you're probably asking in this moment, *a communication device for what*?

This is the question, and the answer, put simply, is the synchronization of your mind, body, and spirit.

If we can synchronize these three components of our holistic being, then we are able to switch on this cosmic love antenna, and then we are able to remember and express and, most important, embody our unique frequency of love.

Only when the synchronization is complete, through the bridging and communication of our emotions,

does this frequency start to expand.

So that is really what we're getting at here, today.

I'm going to be giving you my perspectives, my experiences, and what I've observed in my work

to really show you an example not only of why this energy, emotion, and communication system is important

but how it links us across mind, body, and spirit and how this finally switches on your cosmic love antenna and unique love frequency.

I'll explain it another way because I know that this explanation has really pushed some dominoes over in my being.

Through the traditional Chinese-medicine lens, it is said that a lot of the emotions are connected, and maybe even created, in our organs;

the most famous example, which you might have some experience with, is the liver and its relationship to and creation of anger.

But through this example, I would ask you to go a little bit deeper here.

We can understand through this outline that, "Okay, the liver creates anger.

If I suppress, ignore, or numb that anger, it won't be able to move.

It won't allow that emotion, that *energy in motion*, to move up and out through me. Then, yes, I'm going to have liver challenges."

But let's take a deeper look here; that's why we are connecting the mental and the physical through our experiences.

How is anger generated? Most likely by a thought, a belief, a story that we keep thinking. But take a deeper step and ask yourself, where is that anger, where is that story, where is that belief, where is it originating from?

Is it originating in the physical body or is there a third piece of this puzzle, i.e., the spirit, the soul, which is also playing a role?

As I said a few paragraphs earlier, you are not your emotions, but you are the experience of them, the experiencer that uses the physical body.

So who or what is the experiencer?

The answer to that question, we will talk about later.

For now, I just want you to really sit with this, being for a moment in your soul and spirit.

Through this, it starts to highlight and show the importance of this synchronization of the body, mind, spirit, and the emotional bridge.

If this excites you, if you're starting to make these links, then hold on, because we're going to break these down even more.

And by the end, your beautiful love frequency will be switched on for all to feel and acknowledge.

A powerful understanding I want to help you come to before we get into the beautiful pages ahead is about the role of our subconscious and, more specifically, the emotions that lie within when we're looking to synchronize our mind, body, and spirit,

strengthen our cosmic love antenna, and thus emit our love frequency.

We must understand that our subconscious is not just a head, brain, and mind thing;

your subconscious exists in every piece of your human being.

What this means is that if I have an emotional feeling that I look to heal, to follow, to channel to help me come back to my love frequency,

then this very emotion, which most likely also has a story and a thought attached to it, can exist anywhere in my body, from my pinkie toe to my knee to my stomach, my heart, my throat, and my head,

which is why, in the chapters ahead—when we discuss the chakras, the inner child, the 3D telling a story, your physical pillar, and your heart portal, to name a few—

this will really highlight a beautiful, holistic conversation, and your emotions will be the bridge and the gateway to many of the solutions we're looking to move through.

―――

Another main reason why we want to embrace this mind, body, and soul synchronization

is that it allows us to do something very special.

It allows us to embrace the information that is moving from the outside world into our internal world through the four pathways of interpretation, the four pathways of understanding information.

What do I mean by this?

The powerful Mr. Carl Jung talked about these four consciousness pathways,

which are *thinking, feeling, sensing,* and *intuiting.*

And while I would highly recommend you look up Mr. Jung's work and writings on these four pathways, what I'm going to share here is my experience with them.

When we start to sync the mind, body, and spirit, we now allow these four ways of interpreting information to flow.

Most of us, in this highly mental world that we live in, use only our thinking capacity.

Most of us are not feeling, sensing, or intuiting.

A big reason for this is that we are neglecting our bodies.

A big reason for this is that we are neglecting our spirits and our souls.

The spirit and the soul are two of the pathways in which intuition flows.

The physical body is one of the ways in which our feelings and senses flow.

So you can see how most of us have shut off these pathways and how if we can learn to synchronize and connect our minds, bodies, and spirits, we will have access to these four pathways.

If we have access to these four pathways, we can truly understand the full picture of what is going on in and around us.

For example, beyond just thinking, I can learn to feel in any given situation;

I now have a deeper understanding of how I need to show up.

Another example is that if I can learn to intuit on top of my thinking capacity,

I can now connect to my higher self and my spiritual essence beyond any thinking or thought pattern or belief that might be giving me information.

This is why mind, body, and soul synchronization can be so powerful in not just allowing your love frequency to flow but also in allowing you to show up as the radiant being you were meant to be.

So, to highlight how these four ways of processing, consciousness, and information optimally work in an ideal world,

I want to give an example from my life.

This example is going to show you both the goal and how, unfortunately, most of us are actually getting stuck.

So, with the understanding that we interpret reality through our thinking, through our feeling, through our intuiting and our sensing,

an example in my world that often displays this is when I'm working with a client and channeling either my highest self or a guide, an ancestor, or any loving entity that wants to come through, and how this moves through me is in the following way:

My clairsentience will be activated, which is a spiritual feeling that gives me goosebumps along my skin, and then, based on those goosebumps,

I will get an intuitive download with a message.

I then have emotions expressed from this intuitive download,

and then all of it together is packaged in a thought form or a belief system, which I then share with the client in such a way that they will be able to understand and take in everything from what just moved through me.

Obviously, it doesn't happen in this segmented way; it happens in a few moments, and then I express it with the client,

but this is how it optimally works, to explain it more easily.

I receive intuitive guidance through my intuitive channel.

It expresses through me, through my clairsentience and the goosebumps.

I have an emotional reaction that amplifies and helps me connect more deeply to myself and the person I'm expressing it to,

and then my beautiful, thinking mind helps me package it in a way that's palatable.

This is the optimal, balanced way that we all should function, but for most of us, it doesn't work like this. And there are many ways that this can go wrong.

For example, most of us don't even have our intuition open.

So that guidance coming through, either from that aspect of our higher self or a loving entity, won't even make it through to be perceived.

And even if it is perceived, who's to say that any of our *clair* senses are open—in my example, my clairsentience along my skin was open for me.

Most of us live in very uncomfortable, sick bodies and are not attuned to how our bodies speak to us, let alone how they connect to our spiritual senses.

Then we have the connection to our emotions.

Most of us are suppressing, ignoring, and shutting down our emotional bodies.

And finally, there are our thought patterns.

Unfortunately, as most scientists and professionals now agree, the vast majority of us don't have positive, affirming, and constructive thought patterns.

We have limiting, negative, and deconstructive thought patterns that wrap around this beautiful consciousness we wish to express optimally and authentically.

So you can see how there are many ways in which this whole process can go wrong.

But with divine certainty and some loving intention, this is where this book, your cosmic love antenna, your mind, body, and soul synchronization, and your beautiful love frequency come in.

Part 1
Mind

1
Holding the Inner Child

s we take this deep dive into the first part of the synchronization

and you're coming back to your beautiful love frequency,

I can think of no better place to start than with your beautiful inner child.

I'm not alone when it comes to most of my challenges, pains, and traumas really beginning in those early-childhood years.

Going back to the introduction and the sexual exploration story that I shared,

much of the healing and deeper awareness around that moment in time came not only from my childhood years but also from stepping into the inner child healing process itself, that I now do as an adult with those beautiful inner-child states.

As the wonderful psychologist, self-help author, and inner-child-healer Alice Little states in her books,

"As traumatized children, we always wished someone would come and save us, but we never imagined it would be us as adults."

And that is really what we are doing when we do inner-child healing.

Ideally, our minds should be gardens full of flowers and beautiful beliefs, which are thoughts that we keep thinking that shine bright and empower us and remind us of the gift,

the potential, and the loving inspiration that we actually are.

Unfortunately, that is not the reality for most of us. I know it was not the reality for me,

and my garden, for a very long time, was full of weeds that traced back to this beautiful inner child and the stories I told myself.

Stories that were created around adverse childhood events create our reality.

For example, as a child, I was left at a bus station for hours on end.

I told myself the story that I was alone, that I was abandoned, that I was rejected.

When I was eventually picked up and my beautiful father told me that he purely just forgot,

and that there was just things going on in his life that had taken him away,

at that moment, what would have been best for me to do was to address that story I had created, rewrite it, release it, and move on.

But that's not what happened.

That story was filed away and ended up playing a role in many different situations throughout my adolescence and adulthood.

What we do in inner-child healing from a mental-mind perspective, we now look through our biggest archetypal role,

step into the parent, reparent ourselves, thus rewriting and releasing these stories.

So that child can actually be free. So that child can tune into its natural state of being, which—plot twist—is love.

And we can now actually share ourselves fully, share our frequency fully with the world outside of us.

So, beautiful reader, as you read these words, I encourage you to start bringing some inner-child healing into your world

as the first step on this journey back to your love frequency and to start planting some beautiful seeds that will grow into flowers in the mental scape that is your mind, allowing you to blossom.

―⁓

What is the inner child, anyway?

Well, you can answer this from a couple a couple of different angles,

the first of which is the mental, psychoanalytical, psychological view,

which falls quite squarely into this mind paradigm that we're talking about today.

And through this lens, the inner child is a piece of your inner family constellation or inner family system.

It is the part of you that was rejected, wounded, and left in a traumatized fight-or-flight state from your childhood.

These reactions are most likely being triggered by your relationships in your adult state of being, through your interactions and your adult world.

Through a spiritual lens, in my experience and opinion, the inner child is actually a part of our divinity.

It's a part of our completeness.

I tell clients that the spiritual, divine inner child is the energy and essence of childhood we get to experience in the first years of life: pure bliss, pure joy, and pure play.

What inner-child healing will also help you understand, and this cannot be understated,

is that while your thoughts, much like your beautiful emotions, as we talked about in the introduction,

are communications that you need to listen to and respect while understanding they are not you.

Often, we get stuck in an inner-child story, program, or belief because we feel like we are that story.

We feel like we are the story of "I am rejected."

We feel like we are the story of "I am abandoned."

"I am unlovable."

"I am unworthy."

But this couldn't be further from the truth, and when we start to do inner-child healing and reparent in that garden

and reparent our beautiful little inner being,

we start to see something very significant through a mental-health and mind lens.

We start to see that we are not our thoughts.

We are the essence and the frequency of love that holds them.

Through a mental lens, in this moment, it's important for you to understand that through this inner-child healing,

we start to see these stories, beliefs, and inner-child needs and wounds as aspects of ourselves,

aspects of that greater love frequency that we hold, which you can decide to either nurture or release and let go of.

This is where deep inner-child forgiveness, compassion, and acceptance really come in.

It can be easy to consider the inner child as this broken, wounded, crying little being in the corner.

And while there are definitely layers of fear, pain, and illusion we must move through when holding the child in the mental aspect of your cosmic love antenna, on the road back to your love frequency,

the bigger reality that exists around the inner child is that the child within you is a divine, beautiful, and majestic one.

I will speak to this in more depth in our soulful, spiritual section of the book, but for now,

let me just reiterate and describe for you what the inner-child aspects and the frequency behind them actually are.

The loving, divine inner child—this piece of you is the childlike essence that is untouched, unburdened, and unaffected by the outside fear, illusion, and separation.

Your divine inner child holds the essence of the child consciousness that is waiting for you to let go and fall back into it.

It is almost like the child in the mother's womb, ready to be released and set forth into the world.

This is the inner child of love that will help you express your beautiful love frequency.

Something that starts to occur once you are holding this beautiful inner child within the mental lens on the road back to your love frequency

is the recalibration of an overly masculine way of being.

What I mean by this is that within ourselves and the collective that we belong to,

I and most likely you, the beautiful reader, grew up in a world that is highly masculinized.

What I mean by *masculinization* is the masculine energy within each and every one of us, heavily distorted in this polarity.

What can be noticed is a repression and a pushing down of the feminine, the divine feminine that lies in each of us also.

This divine feminine is responsible for the feeling, the being, and the sensitive release.

The masculine is responsible for the doing, the pushing, the getting-stuff-done.

And while both are vital, as stated, the masculine has a high priority in the world we live in.

I state this here to help you see that by holding the child within this mental structure on the road back to the activation of your cosmic love antenna,

you are filling the role of bringing balance back to the force,

the force of energetic harmony that is needed within the individual and thus the communal whole that we are all part of.

So acknowledge and feel this as you do the work.

One of my favorite inner-child tools, which you can use here, in this moment, was inspired by the famous author, addiction expert, speaker, and physician Gabor Maté.

He references the "seven As of healing" in his writings, and I often use his beautiful guidance in my work,

but in this moment, I want you to focus on the first three.

The first three are acceptance, awareness, and anger.

What I would like to explain now is my flair, perspective, and experience with these important teachings.

We first must accept the story and the belief so we can change it.

We're not accepting its hold on us.

We're not accepting its dysfunction.

We're accepting it so we can make a different choice.

Secondly, we then bring awareness; you are not your thoughts.

What are you? You are the loving frequency that holds and observes the thoughts.

And thirdly, this is where that emotional bridge and link comes in.

We must use our anger or other emotions to allow these stories and beliefs to move up and out of us if they are no longer serving.

Because if we can feel it, we can heal it, and we can move on and let it go.

One of the best ways to start noticing where our beautiful little inner child needs loving attention is to move throughout the day and noticing our triggers,

noticing the spaces and places where we react, where we feel something inside of us move based on something our friend or family member or a lover has said.

The easiest example of this that I can give is when you're on your phone with your mom. How does your energetic being feel?

Or when you just entered the room with your father?

How does the body respond when you go to speak at work in front of your colleagues; what moves through you, and how does your emotional being speak?

Remember, within this mental section of this book, the emotional bridge into your mind is how you feel in any given moment.

And what we can learn to do is to keep tabs on our triggers and see them as gateways back into our salvation.

That emotional response at that family dinner is now the cave that holds the treasure you seek, as the famous author Joseph Campbell states.

So use this practice.

Get into the habit of observing the triggers throughout your day, and what you'll start to notice is a big link to needs that you can start to meet through your inner-child healing.

— —

If we want to start to hold the child and move through our inner-child traumas, challenges, and pain,

one of the best ways we can start to do this is to reclaim our voice.

And what I mean by this is that a big population of us, myself included, as children, were told to shut up and be quiet, to be seen, not heard.

So whether you acknowledge it or not, it is highly likely that you have an unconscious story and belief playing within your mind stopping you from speaking the thing that needs to be said.

And this very deeply connects back to your love frequency; it is stopping you from expressing.

So what is the way that we can move through this?

Well, we can honor our voice and our truth.

One of the biggest challenges that gets in the way of this truth is being concerned and even fearful of how others will perceive us.

So use these steps.

The first tip here is to hone in to your solar plexus, to define and, most important, ask the question, what is your truth?

What is the thing that needs to be expressed in this moment? Feel it; acknowledge it.

Then move it into your chest and your heart space.

Mix that truth with love.

Mix it with compassion and understanding.

Then, finally, step three: move it up into your throat.

And then mix your truth with that love and share it with the world.

Surrender into any fears, any beliefs, any stories that tell you otherwise,

release them, and know that if you have followed these first two steps of definition and the mixture of love,

however your truth is perceived and taken, that is the role of the other person or people in the relationship.

Know that you've done all that you can in expressing your truth,

however it is taken, and that is the other party's role in this beautiful soul contract.

This is how we start to move through and express the thing that needs to be said.

I'd also encourage you to expect the best results. What I mean by this is that most of us don't speak because we fear the worst-case scenario.

However, not many of us are expecting the best-case scenario.

For example, what if you shared your truth and everyone was excited?

Everyone was healed; everyone was inspired by your words.

Stand in this example. Create this reality even before you speak and watch how easy it is to channel your love through your words.

Flowing right on, another powerful tool is the beautiful inner-child letter.

The inner-child letter is exactly what it sounds like.

It is a letter of love to this beautiful little inner child, who deserves to have his or her needs met.

You, as the parent, are reparenting the inner child, so it is your responsibility, your role in this dynamic, to meet the needs.

How can we do this through the letter process?

This letter has three stages. Stage one is connecting to the inner child and honing in on an experience, a memory, or a moment where a need was not met.

The goal of this writing and journaling is to not relive but to release any emotions and stories that are no longer serving you.

You can optimize this by writing with your nondominant hand to connect into the unconscious and subconscious inner-child archetype.

You can add crayons or colored pencils to make it more playful. You could even add essential oils and be out in nature.

Just get writing.

Stage two is reading the letter and using your powerful voice, as we spoke about earlier, to channel any other emotions, any other stories that need to be let go of and released.

When we speak the inner-child letter, we can also visualize ourselves as the parent reading to the inner child that needs to be held.

And finally, stage three of this letter process is reading your inner-child letter in the presence of another person, someone that is holding space for you.

That person is not there to critique, analyze, or judge what you are speaking; they are purely there to create an extra container of healing for you to channel more of your love, more of your healing frequency out into the world.

We often forget that we are spiritual beings but also human animals, and human animals work really well and heal together in tribes.

So when we hold the container for another person in this kind of exercise, it optimizes the energy that needs to move.

So try out this letter today to start to hold the child, align your mental capacity, and allow the love frequency to start to move through you.

— —

The reason why the inner child is such an important component of learning how to emit your unique love frequency through your cosmic antenna of love

is that that most of our challenges, pains, and traumas took place in our childhoods,

and I'm going to get into some other areas in this mind section where traumas can take place, such as down our ancestral lines,

but for the majority of people, the most significant,

apparent challenges you can target to start seeing results immediately are from your childhood.

Many of you reading this book can probably connect to at least one event that seriously shifted your relationship with not just the world outside of you

but the world inside of you.

And this is the point.

If you are disconnected from your internal world due to an external event,

then you are unable to emit this love frequency fully.

And this is exactly why we are doing inner-child healing.

We are parenting that beautiful little inner being that is inside of you right now.

That gorgeous inner child is most likely with you and expressing while reading these words.

It is so significant.

And you do not need years of training.

You do not need to get a certification, to study at school, to begin doing this work.

Don't get me wrong.

It's sometimes necessary to hire an individual—a coach, doctor, or practitioner—to support and guide you so you are safe.

But we all have access to this healing potential,

and this is why inner-child healing is such an important tool in your medicine bag on the road back to your love frequency.

One of the final protocols or tools I can help you with to hold the child and do inner-child healing in this mental part of the path back to your love frequency

lies in two single words: acceptance and forgiveness.

From my experience, acceptance is synonymous with forgiveness, and whether we're using forgiveness or acceptance,

The main point I wish to impart to you is the role of letting go of old paradigms, old stories, old emotions and pain,

the role of accepting where you are now so you can take a step forward—

and please do not get me wrong when I say acceptance.

I'm not condoning any abuse, any perpetrators, any action of others that caused you pain.

What I am saying is that you first need to accept the pain of where you're at so you can alchemize it and change and transform into your future.

So acceptance, forgiveness, and letting go play a very big role in your inner-child healing.

For example, if you have experienced some kind of rejection or abandonment wound with your caregivers,

then there's going to be a piece of you, probably one of your inner children, that is holding on to resentment, judgment, guilt, shame, or anger toward these perpetrators.

So step one is to let go, accept, and forgive.

So you can heal.

Step two, and this will take us a little bit deeper, is that we must accept, forgive, and let go of not just the external blame, shame, and judgment

but also the internal shame, blame, and judgment that we have for ourselves.

If you can accept, let go of, and forgive these pieces, then your inner-child healing and thus the mental parameter of your mind, body, and soul synchronization will start to lighten up, and your love frequency will start to express itself through you.

— —

If you've done any kind of inner-child work before, you've most likely heard the term *attachment style*.

You've also most likely understood the importance of setting healthy boundaries and becoming an individualized being.

I want to speak about now about how both healthy attachment and becoming an individual can be so important within the mental realm of your cosmic love antenna

and how it can lead to expressing more of your love frequency.

Most of us have very unhealthy attachment styles due to trauma, pain, etc.

And because of this and the world that we grew up in,

we are left wounded; we are left insecure and looking for the remedy to make us feel safe.

This stops us from individualizing. If you look at Maslow's hierarchy of needs,

self-individualization and self-actualization are at the top of the pyramid.

Unfortunately, most of us are at the bottom, stuck in a fight-or-flight, unsecure attachment style.

We are looking outside of the self for someone to come and save us.

And this is where we get to the crux of this point and what I wish to share with you.

As referenced above in the powerful Alice Little quote about reparenting,

this shows that, one, we are the answer,

and two, if we're looking to come back to a secure attachment and also become individualized and autonomous in many ways, then again, we are the answer.

Don't get me wrong.

You may need a coach, a therapist, or a practitioner to hold the space needed.

But at the end of the day, it will always be you that meets the need. It will always be you allowing yourself to come back to that healthy attachment and beautiful self-actualization and realization that you deserve to have.

So hold this understanding in your heart because it will allow the inner child to be nurtured, and it will also allow your love frequency to start being emitted from your being.

2

The Ancestral Breaker of Chains

s I have walked through my own ancestral healing on the road back to the activation of my cosmic love antenna

and my beautiful love frequency,

I've remembered and reawakened past events.

And when I say *events*, and when I use the umbrella term of *ancestral healing*,

I refer to events that are both down my family line, down my mother's or father's line or in my past lives.

I've noticed, through the work that I've done on myself and with the clients, that often our past lives recur down our family lines. So these two types of healing, past life and family line, are synonymous.

I bring up these two examples because as I alluded to, in my journey, whether it's been through events around Atlantis,

around The Salem witch trials, or around much cultural religious persecution,

there is much trauma and pain in my ancestral line that is waiting to be healed and moved through.

This same ancestral pain and trauma is also in front of my beautiful love frequency.

If this is so for me, it is most likely so for you too.

If this resonates as you read these words and you're getting a little bit emotional, that is a sign in itself that this type of inner dynamic exists for you.

So I share my own experience to help you to start brainstorming around this as we go deeper into this chapter.

As you read these tips and tools, notice again how they make you feel, because most of these ancestral chains are unconscious,

and by their nature, they are sitting under the surface, and by reading these pages, you are bringing conscious awareness to these unconscious ancestral chains, which now finally have the light of day in which to be seen, felt, and healed.

— —

When you start to do ancestral healing and become the breaker of chains in many ways,

you're starting to take your power back.

Much like the inner child within the first mental structure of our synchronization and emitting our love frequency,

this paradigm and healing pathway helps you reclaim the parts of you that are in trauma, paralyzed by fear, beliefs, and dense, heavy emotions,

but this time, instead of these stories, beliefs, and emotions stemming back to childhood,

these traumatized aspects are now following the branches and roots of your family tree,

whether it's your mother's or your father's line.

That which is unhealed is passed on. It is said that we, as children, take up the responsibility and the role of healing that which is left unhealed by our parents.

And when we do ancestral healing, we start to really lean into this beautiful opportunity.

It is an opportunity because we aren't just healing for the sake of healing when we do ancestral healing.

When we start to pull back these layers within the ancestral tree and become the breaker of chains we deserve to be,

we reclaim our light, and we start to emit our love frequency.

This is because many of our ancestral wounds, pains, and traumas, which have been passed down, are ancient.

Not only are these wounds and pains ancient, but they also have a heavy hold on our minds, our bodies, and our souls.

Here in this mental part of our journey back to love:

you must understand that while the stories and beliefs did not originate with us,

it is now our light that can unravel them.

As an example, I've noticed that my interaction with my sexuality and my beautiful feminine nature of sensitivity and emotion doesn't just live in me.

I've noticed parts of this both in my mother's and my father's lines, and the more I've started to heal this and lean into this and emit my love frequency,

the more I've noticed that it's impacted not just me but also individuals in those same mother and father lines.

So I share this as an example to help you, the beautiful reader, see the power of this and how it fits into the mental structure

and how you can become this breaker of chains.

Once we start to acknowledge these negative thought forms, these stories and beliefs,

and start to rewrite them and release them, the heaviness that they hold starts to lighten up,

and we're able to create a new reality and start thinking and believing from an expanded place rather than a limiting place.

One of my favorite practices for doing this kind of ancestral healing work within your inner mental world

is to start tuning into each of your energy centers, or chakras, individually, from your crown down to your root.

As you do this, bring either your mother or father into your mind's eye as you connect to each of these different areas of the body.

What you can do is start to notice how your internal state and physicality feels, how your chest feels, how your stomach feels, how your throat feels.

Do you notice any tension, any resistance, any pain, as you observe them and move down the different chakras?

If you notice pain, breathe into it,

releasing and letting go of anything that might come up.

What are the stories, beliefs, or old patterns that might be playing out?

As you observe your mother and father in each of these different energy centers and through the body,

is their age staying the same or changing?

Is there anything else that bubbles up?

Are there further stories, further beliefs that move through you in this moment?

There are probably emotions too.

So what you can do through your mental capacity is to acknowledge and release the emotions—

but in this moment, decide to make a choice to rewrite any stories, any beliefs that have come up in the presence of your mom or your dad in each energy center.

This exercise can be repeated with many kinds of ancestors and shows you the power of your mind but also the power of your choice to let go and become the breaker of chains of any belief, thought, or program that no longer serves you.

One of the most common ancestral chains that we can learn to break, which I've noticed within my own ancestral line

and in those of many people that have come to see me, involves holding on and storing emotions and feelings of guilt and shame.

There are many events, stories, and beliefs that attach themselves to guilt and shame that we then store in our beings.

By purely bringing this into your awareness and starting to look through this lens of guilt and shame down your ancestral line,

you will start to become aware of many examples in your own storyline of situations, memories, or traumatic events through your parents, your grandparents, or even further back.

For example, many of us have grown up surrounded by a lot of religious views and beliefs.

And I want to preface what I'm about to say with the compassionate view that I believe in all the world religions; there are many loving and mystical foundations in all of them.

However, I've come to realize that there are a lot of manmade layers on top of all the world religions that lead to a lot of fear, suppression, repression, and trauma.

Two of the most common emotions created by this religious trauma are guilt and shame.

So with this very example, we can start to look for these religious traumatic events that we're holding on to guilt and shame around, down our ancestral line, which we deserve to be the break of chains of.

One very specific example is your sexual expression.

As a little boy who grew up in a religious context,

I felt great guilt and shame around exploring my sexual identity,

whether it be sexual touch, masturbation, or exploring the bodies of others due to religious teachings.

I felt guilty; I felt shameful for doing so.

Does this resonate with you?

Do you have similar stories and beliefs and experiences? Because if so, then you have a chain to break, which would help you to not only release these emotions and rewrite these thought forms and stories

but also to hone in on your internal love frequency.

A beautiful way that we can start to optimize our ancestral healing and start to see what needs to be broken and brought into loving, healing awareness

is by opening our hearts and sending out the invitation to bring in our ancestral guides.

This ability is something that we all have, yet most of us do not use it.

When we're looking to be the breaker of our ancestral chains, we must understand that our ancestors want us to break these chains just as much as we want to.

So what you can learn to do within your meditations, breathwork, nature immersion or any other practice that helps you open up to your spiritual life

is to add ancestral connection to it and bring in these exact loving entities.

For me, what this looks like is closing my eyes, putting my hands on my heart, and simply requesting assistance and guidance from my ancestors,

both down my ancestral line and on the land that I live on.

The simple intention and the simple prayer that we make with this can help us to heal.

It can also help us move through this mental sphere within our mind, body, and soul synchronization on the road back to releasing our love frequency with our cosmic love antenna.

So practice this ancestral prayer today.

Remember that they respect your free will, and while they want you to heal just as much as you want to heal, you have to ask for the assistance you deserve first.

— —

Much like inner-child healing, ancestral healing is a core pillar in pulling back the layers to emit your frequency of love.

The reason I say this and feel this and have had experience with this is that once we've started to move through our inner-child wounds,

we then realize very quickly that a lot of these pains didn't start with us.

For example, if I have uncovered an inner-child wound of abandonment or rejection or humiliation

that has been exacerbated or caused by one of my parents,

I can, without a doubt, point out in that same parent almost the exact same wound or a very similar one from their childhood.

And this is where ancestral healing comes in.

If we can make the link between inner-child healing and the ancestral line and the wounds, the pains, and the traumas that are passed down,

this simple awareness can take your healing to a deeper level because you're becoming the breaker of chains, healing generations of inner-child wounds and thus exponentially increasing your ability to emit your love frequency.

Another example here:

if I can break the limiting belief that has been passed down my generations that boys aren't emotional

or men aren't sensitive,

I'm not only healing me, but I'm evoking and bringing in all of the ancestors that had that same wound, and this now magnifies my love frequency.

This propels my chances and ability to share this frequency with the world because I have a whole team, a whole tribe, a whole family behind me.

This is the importance of ancestral healing within this love-frequency conversation.

Another tip and protocol I'm going to prescribe for you in this ancestral-healing chapter is the role of tribe,

specifically the role of tribe in this ancestral context.

For a moment, I want you to follow a thought process with me.

Throughout this chapter, we will highlight that you are a powerful spiritual being, yes,

but you are also a beautiful human being, a human animal.

This human animal that you are has evolved for thousands of years in tribes and communities whose main function was to evolve and expand together.

Whenever an individual was going through some kind of pain, challenge, or trauma across their mind, body, and spirit,

the tribe would come together and soothe, educate, and help that individual expand.

And this is where we can use the next tool of tribe to help us break not just these ancestral chains and traumas and thought patterns and beliefs that have been passed down

but many of our wounds overall.

This is healing in itself because most of us, as the human animals that we are, don't live like this anymore.

Most of us are living solemnly, in confined houses, by ourselves, separated.

We then ask the question, why is there so much anxiety and depression?

My contention is that this is one of the biggest reasons.

We know that in the blue zones around the world, one of the indicators of longevity is connection among flourishing social groups.

So my point here and the tool I share with you is to bring about and connect to community and tribe around you, not just to heal your ancestral wounds and overcome trauma, limiting thought patterns, and programming that has been passed down the ancestral line

but to overcome many of the other challenges identified in this book.

Tribe heals, but first you must invite it in and welcome its loving embrace.

― ―

Being the breaker of ancestral chains and doing this ancestral healing work on the road back to your love frequency isn't all pain and shadow.

What I'd love to share with you now is a beautiful opportunity and invitation that you can step into.

When you do this ancestral healing work, you are sending a signal down your ancestral line,

and this signal is one of hope, compassion, healing, and love.

What I mean by this is that there are many studies now being done in the field of parapsychology showing that when someone is moving through something painful and traumatic,

such as many of the types of healing we've talked about in this exploration thus far,

our spiritual support team—more specifically, our ancestors, who are very much alive in the ancestral plane—is most active around us.

So ancestral healing can also mean not only calling to ancestors who are there waiting to give you their love but also acknowledging that they love you unconditionally and want to support you through the pain most of all.

These ancestors want you to heal this trauma, this pain, this limiting belief, this soul loss as much as you want to heal it.

So step into this power and remembrance the next time you're doing any of this work,

and I think you'll be very surprised not only by who shows up but by how strong the force of love is behind them and their healing gifts.

A big hurdle to overcome within your ancestral breaking of chains is a concept and a lesson around soul contracts.

And while there are many teachings, books, lessons, and worldviews on what a soul contract is,

I want to take a moment to explain it in reference to your ancestral healing and the bigger topic of coming back to your inner frequency of love.

I would define a soul contract as a predetermined relationship within any given lifetime to help you and another person or multiple people move through a particular lesson.

And with this understanding, our ancestral healing becomes even more important because it is often down our ancestral line that many of us have, at the very least, a couple of very pivotal and important soul contracts that need to be fulfilled.

Now, what also must be understood is that the nature of reality, in my experience, is one of unconditional love.

God equals unconditional love.

So in this reference to soul contracts down your ancestral line,

there is no judgment; there is no blame, shame, or expectation about whether these soul contracts will be fulfilled.

However, if they're not learned, if they're not moved through, then they will repeat.

So what this leaves us with is an understanding and an acceptance that most of our ancestral wounds, traumas, pains, and challenges have been seen before and are now waiting for you to unlock them.

So whether it is through connecting to your ancestors, through any of the tools and healing practices we've talked about thus far,

when you break an ancestral chain, you are also leaning into a beautiful soul contract,

and through a mental lens, this allows us to overcome a lot of the limiting beliefs, stories, and neural pathways that are keeping us stuck and small.

3
The Healthy Ego

ow that we understand the necessity of starting to become the breakers of chains and the healers of inner children in our mental worlds,

we can see what is getting in the way for us,

which is having—or most likely not having—something that is referred to as a healthy ego.

If we are looking to enhance, define, and ultimately emit our unique frequency of love to change ourselves,

to change others and eventually change the world,

we have to make sure that our egos are healthy.

Within certain mental, emotional, and spiritual communities and groups, the ego gets a bad rap. You hear phrases such as:

"We need to kill the ego!"

"We need to destroy the ego!"

And in my experience on my journey, this could not have been more disastrous, for the ego is our beautiful self-expression.

It is the little "I" or the little self that deserves just as much expression as the big self inside of us.

Thus we must understand that we're not here to kill the ego.

We are here to love the ego and make it a healthy space of expression so we're not projecting our wounds, our traumas, and our pains

but expressing our unique frequency fully through a space of expansion, lightness, and ultimately, love.

— —

So the next question that probably arises in you is, "Okay, how do I do that?"

Well, the short answer is that we've already been moving through this,

both through inner-child healing and becoming the ancestral breaker of chains.

The big reason for this is that your inner-child wounds and ancestral chains are mostly what cause the ego to be unhealthy to begin with.

If you are moving through the guidance we've talked about thus far, you now allow your ego to be integrated; you allow that child to be safe, and you allow those ancestral chains to be broken.

So what you express through yourself, through the ego lens, is of pure love, light, and ultimately, divinity.

But through a mental lens, what you are now doing is becoming balanced.

Within psychoanalytical and psychological realms, you're becoming *securely attached*.

You're allowing your truest potential and your beautiful love frequency to be expressed

without triggers, without traumas, without rejection wounds,

without abandonment, without that story,

without the unhealed mother line, and without that negative belief down your father line.

When we take away and heal and bring the shadows back into the light through the healing processes that we've talked about,

you now express more of your light, more of your love frequency.

And this is where your rubber really meets the road

because through this mental part of your synchronization, you start to realize that your external reality is created by your internal world,

your beliefs, and your feelings, as are the actions that you then take based on them.

—⁓

Your ego, put very simply, is a complex of thoughts, stories, and belief systems.

The latter is what I wish to speak to in this moment.

Because if you can understand this, then you can shift to a healthy ego.

A belief system is inherently closed.

So if you have been raised within a certain religion, within a certain culture, within a certain family or peer group that has stories, thoughts, and beliefs

that were told and projected onto you,

you are in a closed system, which is very difficult to see beyond.

The analogy that I give is that the frog in the well knows nothing of the ocean.

You are the frog in the well that sees its world purely for what the closed belief system says it is.

You can move beyond these belief systems (we will talk more about this in the spiritual chapter), but for now,

just understand that your belief systems do not own you.

To break free of these closed systems, we must see the world not just through our mind, because if we look only through the mind then we look only through these closed systems.

So for now, beautiful reader, hold on to the understanding that if you are stuck within a certain story, certain beliefs, certain ways of thinking,

then this is where you must move from the head to the heart,

seeing just how large your reality actually is.

On this path you are taking toward a healthy ego, in your mental paradigm of the synchronization of your cosmic love antenna and the expansion of your love frequency,

the words *health* and *healthy* come up a lot.

Your ego likes to play a game with these words.

I've noticed on my journey, for example, that I'm always getting stuck in not being healthy enough.

If I am not in a state of vibrant health, I must need to keep pushing,

keep doing,

keep healing, and this is a big obstacle and a challenge.

We all must face what it really means to be healthy.

I wish to share a deeper reflection with you now.

I wish to reframe and help you see health from another angle.

What if health were not a state of lack of pain or disease or challenges

but a state of acceptance and understanding that whatever you're given,

that state of being is for your greatest good in the moment,

allowing you to be more as you step toward the goals and the healing and the transformation that you deserve?

What if that were healthy?

What if being healthy were understanding that there was no right or wrong, only stagnation or expansion?

If we can flip health to be a constant evolution rather than an "I'll be happy when" type of deal, then health becomes a process rather than an outcome that will always be replaced with another outcome.

I hope this finds your heart, because if this shift within the ego can be made, then a lot of expectations and unnecessary stress and pressure can be removed.

Another tool to support the journey back to a healthy ego within the mental element of your cosmic love antenna is learning to raise your frequency before moving through and alchemizing a shadow aspect.

This is important because as we have seen with the moving through of our inner child aspects, our ancestral aspects,

all of the wounds and the pain that our ego often holds on to,

we must learn to raise our frequency to one of love if we wish to move through the shadows effectively.

I big understanding and reason for raising our frequency before moving through our shadows is because what often occurs is that we either identify with those shadows, emotions, beliefs, and stories

or we tend to run away and suppress them.

Neither option is enough to move through to the gifts, the love frequency, and ideally to integrate and heal the shadows within the ego.

So we must raise our frequency.

How can we raise our frequency?

This will be individualized and unique to each soul.

For me, for example, it looks like grounding on the earth,

adding in some wholesome food, moving my body, chanting and connecting to chakra cleansing.

So, beautiful being, what raises your frequency?

What lifts your multidimensional being upward so you can look and hold the space for the shadows that need to be moved through?

— —

An additional element to consider with the ego is it being the flipside of the soul that you are.

A role and responsibility that the ego has is to search for and find separation

so that you, as the powerful being that you are, can alchemize this separation back into oneness and your beautiful love frequency.

I share this again to help you remove any judgment, any shame, any guilt over catching your ego doing something "wrong."

The ego is doing exactly what it needs to do.

It is our added perception and judgment on this act that leads us down into more separation.

We add judgment to the judgment. We add guilt to the guilt, anger to the anger, shame to the shame,

when ideally we need to observe,

we need to observe the ego doing its job beautifully and decide to make a different choice.

Instead of leaning into the separation with more separation,

we can lean in with our love to construct a healthy ego and then step forward beyond the fear, the pain, and the separation itself.

Yet another thorn in the ego that stops us from constructing a healthy self-expression lens

is the emotion and feeling of envy.

For me, this has often come up within my relationships, my business, and my expansion of financial abundance.

I found it very easy, in my past, to be envious of other people that had certain things that I wanted.

I saw them and become envious, and then, in that act, I was in many ways telling myself that I didn't deserve what they had.

Because if we live in a reality,

where we accept that we are all beautiful mirrors and reflections of each other,

the moment that I become envious of another is the same moment I am telling myself, *I do not deserve that.*

So the point and the loving guidance I wish to share with you around envy and creating a healthy ego

is to start to see envy as something we can release but also alchemize into celebration,

into motivation and inspiration.

As an example, every time I catch myself feeling envious for something outside of me,

I flip it and turn it into excitement.

An even more specific example: each time I see someone that has a business, financial, or relationship element that I want,

I celebrate them, because the moment I celebrate them, I'm also celebrating my potential to reach the same outcome.

Now we are starting see the power of the mental sphere of the synchronization journey back to your loving frequency.

You can see the power in that through your healthy ego and the reintegration of the balanced mental sphere,

what you are creating internally and thus projecting externally is a reality in which you are expansive and can fully show up as your fullest expression.

— —

Something that's very important to understand with your healthy ego is that the ego in itself is not innately good or bad,

which at this point it should be starting to become clear,

while also understanding that

it is a lens of expression.

Ultimately, what we wish to do is to project our love frequency through this individual expression for the entire world to see.

Most of us are walking around with a lot of ego masks that leave us feeling small.

For example, many of us go to jobs we don't like,

put on a title we don't want,

and express ourselves through this ego lens, asking ourselves the question and being left wondering, *Why do we not feel expanded?*

So what we can learn to understand is that if the current ego mask is not leading to our love frequency emitting more into the world,

we can ask the question, *How much deeper into myself do I need to go?*

How much deeper through my mental healing, my physical healing and my spiritual healing do I need to go to allow my truest expression to filter through my ego lens?

So now we work with our ego rather than against it.

───

I've noticed on my journey and in many of the journeys of the of the individuals I've been able to support

that whenever we start to have a conversation around a healthy ego, then neural pathways, memory healing, subconscious reprogramming, and cognitive behavioral therapy—

all of these terms and healing pathways come up.

And I would like to address them here to connect them to the larger topic of your love frequency, your mind-body-soul synchronization, and your cosmic love antenna.

Through the mental lens, your neural pathways are connected to your thoughts and beliefs.

A belief is a thought that you keep thinking, just to make that clear.

And often, our thoughts, beliefs, and stories are the neural pathways that keep firing over and over, allowing us to create the reality we choose to be in.

And ideally this would be beautiful.

However, most of us are creating a reality from a space of pain, from a space of disconnection trauma, from our past and fear.

So what we want to ask is how we start to reprogram or rewire or create new neural pathways to allow new thoughts, new beliefs, new stories, and a new reality.

An analogy and image I want to share with you to describe all this is the beautiful snowy mountain.

The snowy mountain is your brain, the neural scape in which all of your neural pathways have the possibility of forming.

Each time you walk down the mountain, you create a new path, a new thought, and new neural pathway.

Each time we walk down the snowy mountain on that same path, the path gets deeper, to the point that you cannot walk down that entire mountain without going down that same path.

This is the belief.

This is the story.

This is the thought that we often get stuck in, especially if it is one that we do not want, a negative belief and thought.

So we must learn to see that the reason it is so hard to get out of this way of thinking is that the path is so deep in the snow.

And just because we're deep in the snow, it does not mean the rest of the mountain does not exist.

So this is where a lot of tools, practices, and healing across mind, body, and spirit come in to help us rewire, reprogram, and move out of the snowy path, stepping into the rest of our potential.

———

A very important understanding around coming back to a healthy ego is the power we have to create our reality.

As I've stated in this chapter, the ego is not innately good or bad.

It is a screen or a lens of expression we project ourselves through.

Most of us are projecting our wounds, our inner-child trauma, and our ancestral chains and creating our reality through them.

This leaves us feeling demoralized, like we are the victim.

However, what we can learn to understand is that we are truly the creators of our reality.

And once we start to heal and unwind and take our power back and connect to not just the cosmic love antenna we are but the frequency of love that moves through us,

we can create the reality we deserve.

We can remember the innately creative beings that we have always been.

We were born to cocreate with the external universe that is connected to us intrinsically and create evolution and expansion.

We were born as the individual soul expressions that we are to connect to our love frequency, which is often associated with fulfillment, happiness, pleasure, and joy, to the external canvas

and create an evolutionary environment that is beneficial not just to the individual but to all.

So as you read these words, I hope they remind you that through the activation of your love frequency

and its expression through your healthy ego,

you create a reality that is expansive, compassionate, accepting, and most of all, loving.

Back to another method for you to use within this understanding of a healthy ego, and it is one of my favorite words: awareness.

I'm going to quote one of my teachers now.

And that is the powerful new-age author, scientist, visionary and scholar Mr. Gregg Braden.

Gregg Braden teaches:

"The act of observation is an act of creation unto itself."

I would like for you to read this sentence a few times over.

What this shows us, in many ways, is the power of the observer effect. The observer effect, through the quantum physics lens, means, very simply, that the act of observing anything in our reality changes it.

So in relation to our minds, our egos, and more specifically, our unconscious trauma loops

and the conscious healing we seek to step into when we purely observe that which we want to change—it changes it.

So, what is an example of this?

Well, an example would be catching that negative thought pattern that's telling you that there is no way that you can express your love frequency.

Another example would be observing that wounded little inner child that we spoke about in our inner-child chapter and purely observing him or her from a space of love.

This act of observation and awareness changes your internal terrain.

And I've noticed with the beautiful clients I have been able to support that this in itself can be enough to shift.

This is also why when you start to implement a regular meditation practice, when you start to connect into the observer or the big self

and start healing your ego, most of this is done through the act of observation or awareness.

The good news is that you most likely have been doing this already throughout these pages,

so continue to practice in your day today and lean into this loving creation act.

One very important component of a healthy ego is to rewrite and release the belief that any kind of self-care or self-love that we do is selfish.

Throughout this book,

it's important to see a lot of the tools and practices and guidance that I share as many different kinds and forms of self-love.

If we see them this way on our road back to our love frequency expression,

then we must break free from the belief that any kind of self-love is selfish.

We must learn to put "I" before groups and the whole and, in the act of doing this, remember that this is a way of being of service.

We cannot express our light and love to the world if our cup is either empty or does not know how to pour.

When we do any of the work and the healing and the practices throughout this book, it helps us express and turn on our light.

It is from this space we can then step out into the world and share said light.

So in the act of putting ourselves first, we are actually helping others.

In the act of releasing, expressing, healing, and diving deeper into oneself,

we are helping the world by turning on more of our frequency, and this frequency needs to be felt, seen, and experienced by as many people as possible.

So before you go any further, please rewrite the belief that self-love is selfish and exchange it with the belief that self-love is selfless—a way that you help the collective expand.

—— ——

Shifting out of the archetype of the victim is a game changer when it comes to starting to unlock your healthy ego.

In the previous chapters, we have already talked about this within the mental healing paradigm, specifically in reference to your ancestral chains and your inner child trauma. Within both of these categories, it's very easy to get stuck as the victim.

The victim is the one who sees that their pain, their challenges, and their external circumstances are happening to them,

and they are the victim of unforeseeable, unchangeable, and undetermined situations.

And while most would see this as reality—

I know I did for a very long time—

it is my belief and perspective that we not only live in a universe where everything is happening for a reason, but we live in a universe where everything's happening for us.

So a pivotal position and shift to make within the mental structure of building a healthy ego once more

is understanding that you are not the victim.

You attract what you are.

This goes for the beautiful, positive, and loving elements in your life.

And this also goes for the painful experiences.

Be careful with my words here.

I'm not saying that the people, places, and things involved in these painful circumstances do not need to take responsibility;

they do, but who else needs to take responsibility?

You do, and if you have an ancestral chain or an inner-child trauma that is left unhealed,

you will attract people, places, and things that continue to help you see this wound so you can heal it.

So understand this shift out of being the victim, and move from being the damaged, wounded soul

to the empowered, transformational healer.

— —

Again, sharing a bit of my own story here now.

When I'm in this mode (healthy ego), I'm in pure creation energy.

Let me be very clear with my words.

There is no such thing as "Harrison is creative and you, the reader, are not."

We are all creative beings; we are made of creation energy, and in many ways this creation energy is the same as your love frequency.

So when we have a healthy ego that we are projecting our creation energy and love frequency through,

then the world and ultimately even the universe is our oyster.

This is because our love frequency is one of abundance.

Through our healthy ego we are now creating via abundance, what we want to manifest

and our internal thought world now expresses itself fully, with positivity.

Instead of having stories and beliefs of limitation and unprocessed emotions take us away and stopping us from taking certain actions,

we are now in a state of being encouraged as we are,

following the bliss we are,

following the expansion we are,

and bringing our love frequency into the spaces and places we need it to be not just for our own evolution

but for the evolution of the greater collective.

And I don't know about you, but this is a frequency, this is a way of being, that I want more of.

So as we wrap up this mind section of your synchronization journey back to your love frequency,

hold this feeling in your field and in your heart.

If you can hold it there, then the next categories, the body and the soul, will fall into place.

Part 2
Body

4
The 3D Tells a Story

s a teenage boy, I was sexually abused.

I share this as we start this chapter to highlight not just the importance of the words to come

but also the necessity of coming back to this deeper love frequency.

As I shared at the beginning of this book, as a little boy, I was confused by my inner feminine energy and the relationship to my sensitivities.

And due to this, I suppressed, pushed down, and ignored parts of my feminine nature.

Fast-forward to this teenage event.

I remember vividly being in a teenage-party setting, having a bit too much to drink, and winding up by myself in a dark room, trying to sleep.

It was here, through my drunken blacking in and out,

that I remember a larger man coming into the room I was sleeping in and subsequently touching, forcing himself on, and taking advantage of me.

It took me a long time to be able to express and talk about this event, let alone to write and share about it in public settings like this one.

But I felt it would be valuable to share with you, beautiful reader, because not only did that moment highlight exactly how the 3D tells a story

and how that emotionally, physically, mentally, and even spiritually abusive act continued for days, months, and years after as I ignored, suppressed, and pushed it down,

but there was also a deeper meaning behind it.

I now realize that part of my feminine energy wanted it to be felt and experienced.

And this is by no means condoning and justifying the act.

The perpetrator deserves to be held accountable and to take responsibility for the actions that he stood in.

And I also understand that hurt people hurt people.

What I'm getting at here is that as the boy that I was, if my journey had been different,

if my sensual, feminine, and ultimate love frequency was flowing from the start,

then I feel this adolescent event would have gone very differently.

And again, I share this to inspire you to ask the question,

How has the pain in my life come to show me something deeper?

In this chapter, we will answer this question together through the 3D and the body telling a story of your life.

— —

As we take our next big, beautiful step into the second part of our mind, body, and soul synchronization on the road back to your beautiful love frequency,

we now dive into your amazing body, which I will be referring to often as the "3D".

Much like how in the mental scape our emotions were the bridge from the mental to the physical,

the same emotions are the bridge into the deeper layers of the physical being.

This is because when we experience a trauma, a pain, a challenge from our past that is restricting our loving light

or restricting our full mind-body synchronization,

it isn't just coming with a limiting belief or limiting story; it's coming with an emotion that is trapped in the physical body.

So this is the first understanding about this bridge: that if I, for example, to go back to our exploration around all things inner child,

experienced an inner-child abuse in that created a belief that I was not worthy, at that moment in time, that unworthy belief also created a feeling of potential sadness, a feeling of potential grief, a feeling of potential anger.

But then, where was that story and that emotion trapped?

Well, this is where we now take this next chapter deeper.

Both that belief and that emotion were trapped in the body.

This is where the 3D and your physical body tell a story.

I am one of many to highlight this emotional-mental-physical link. Another powerful statement and resource underlining all of this is the very famous phrase *The Body Keeps the Score*, the title of a book by the beautiful, best-selling trauma author, researcher, and educator Bessel Van der Kolk.

It depicts this very understanding that our traumas, our pains, and our abuses, if left unhealed, unintegrated, and unreleased, will leave our beautiful bodies to "keep the score," in his words—giving us the opportunity to eventually let go and to heal.

The question that comes up here is how, exactly, we start to move through this.

⁓ ⁓

To answer this question, we have to put a slight pause on one particular topic that we'll come back to later, and that is the energetic chakra system.

But while we wait to come back to that in the next chapters, what we can start with is an understanding that our mind and the space and place in which we hold onto pains, challenges traumas, stories, and emotions

is not just a brain or a head thing.

It is a full-body conversation.

So if we can understand and conceptualize this, we can target particular areas of the body

to bring awareness, attention, deeper healing, and release to the 3D telling a story.

Not because it's holding on to judgment toward us,

not because it wants to keep us within the victim mindset.

But because it inevitably and innately loves us.

It's depicting the novel of our lives in a very chronic fight-or-flight state, and how this looks for most people is constantly being hypervigilant, looking outside of oneself for the tiger,

for the abuser, for the traumatic event that's coming to get us, and while this is good in the short term,

and this is good for keeping us safe from retraumatizing ourselves in the long term,

it leads to very stressed-out beings that are definitely not in their bodies and are always looking outside of themselves.

The reason that this is so important to understand is that if we are looking to connect to our internal love frequency,

let alone synchronize the mind, body, and spirit,

it cannot be done from an external location of the self.

It can be done only by inner exploration.

So this is where we must learn to release the stories, beliefs, and trapped emotions through the body itself.

In this moment now, I want to bring your attention to two very powerful exercises and tools.

The first of which is once again your loving attention or awareness.

When we can simply observe an emotion, a story, or a thought in the body that's coming up in any given moment,

what we need to do is to become something I call the container of love.

In meditative circles, this is called becoming the loving observer.

Same name for the same act.

Whenever we bring our objective, loving attention to the emotion that we feel in a particular area of the body or a story playing over and over, which usually comes with a sensation,

we detach and de-identify ourselves from the emotion, from the thought, from the belief.

When we do this, we're able to move through it.

We're able to let it go; we're able to release; we are able to move on, and this is where tool number two comes in.

Once we've brought our loving attention or awareness to the emotion, the feeling, the thought in the body,

we want to create space to let it flow.

We want to create space to let it be released, and what is the best way we can do this?

One word: breath.

When we intentionally use our breath and breathe into a particular area of the body, that's holding an emotion or a belief,

we are doing a few different things.

First of all, we're creating the space for that emotion and thought to flow, to move, to be acknowledged and let go of,

and we're also bringing in the love that's outside of us.

In that very moment in time, what we can understand is that the loving power that we're looking to tap into inside of us is also outside of us.

As within, so without.

So what we can learn to do, visually, is to close our eyes.

Imagine that we're breathing in love.

Direct that love to the area of the body where we feel the emotion, the pain, the tension, and then imagine ourselves breathing out that resistance.

Breathing out that emotion, breathing out that limiting belief or that thought form that no longer serves us.

When we combine loving attention and awareness with the power of love through the breath, we now have a perfect one-two combo

to release the 3D from telling its story of pain, to come back into this present moment and emit more of our divine love frequency.

Let's take a moment now and go even deeper into this understanding of the body holding on and the emotional release that occurs during this process.

Let's pinpoint and hone in on the emotion and feeling of grief.

Grief is probably one of the most common expressions and releases that occur once we start going into our tissues and our physical bodies to let go and release the stored emotion that is inhibiting the expression of our love frequency.

What I want to encourage you to do is to accept the power of love to help us move through grief.

Just like we expressed when we talked about holding the inner child, love and grief can go together.

When you are in a feeling and an embodiment of grief,

that is when you can love yourself the most. We are not loving to push the grief away; we are not loving to increase the speed with which the grief moves through us;

we are loving because love can allow the grief to be fully felt when we embrace ourselves in a moment of sadness and grief.

We are accepting the grief and ourselves in all that we are, and this is powerful.

This is also helping us embody more of our love frequency in the act of emotional grief itself.

So when grief arises, take the opportunity to love and connect your love frequency to the grief process in its entirety.

I want to give another example of how the body stores trauma and one way we can start to release and heal.

This is also a beautiful example of the emotional bridge's components, which are now rippling into the physical body.

If you have experienced some kind of traumatic event, let's say in childhood, and during that childhood event,

some emotion was experienced—

let's use the example of anger—

if you were like me, in many situations, maybe you were told not to express your anger.

Maybe you were told that it's too much to express your anger.

It's not manly to express your emotions. You must hold it in, push it in, ignore it, and store it.

Then what happens is that the anger doesn't disappear.

What is emotion? Emotion is energy in motion. So that anger and energy flows and is stored in the body; your tissues hold your issues.

So what we can learn to do now is, bring awareness to this—because remember, the act of awareness is an act of creation in itself.

Creative energy helps us to heal and release.

But what we can also do is to learn to understand through the physical body what a healthy expression of anger is.

Referencing once again the famous author, addiction expert, speaker, and physician Gabor Maté, he teaches about what healthy, balanced anger is.

Like all emotions, anger is unbalanced when we repress it and store it, as in this example,

or it's unbalanced when we take it out as rage on a person, place, or thing,

but we forget that there is a balanced, healthy expression of anger.

And we channel that anger up and out through the body, through the voice, through movement, and through our words,

and we let it flow. That is when we stand in our anger, not directing it, not numbing it, not storing it, and allow it to move through us.

Now we are not only balancing the anger but also releasing the body from storing anything, allowing the emotion to move and letting go of pain that is most likely showing up as other physical symptoms.

Much like I've been discussing in previous chapters the importance of ancestral healing, inner-child healing, and the other themes in relationship to their importance for starting to express your love frequency,

your 3D telling the story of your life and the trauma it keeps track of in your tissues is also in the same boat.

Dear reader, I want you to know that I'm not just picking random topics out of my medicine bag to include in this adventure.

They all have an intention, and the intention of the 3D telling a story in relationship to your love frequency is vast.

It is vast because you cannot stand in your love frequency if your body is constantly reacting to and being triggered by stored emotions, stories, and beliefs.

As you step out into the world, you cannot express your love frequency when you go to speak on stage, in your business, or at an event

if you have an old trauma, belief, or pain from your past stuck in your solar plexus or your chest or your throat, which is keeping you in a fight-or-flight state,

a state of fear that stops you from speaking the thing that needs to be said.

This very simple example shows that if we're not constantly aware of how our bodies are storing and holding onto all of these elements, and we are not processing and releasing and holding space for this energy to move,

then we are limiting ourselves, and conversely, if we create the space, if we do the somatic release, do the breath work,

do the forgiveness work, do all of not just the physical elements in this chapter but also the mental and the spiritual aspects,

we will be able, through the physical, to emit our love frequency in all of the spaces and places we deserve to.

This is your superpower, but most do not acknowledge it.

As we go deeper and deeper into the release of your body and all that it holds on to, what is most likely to occur?

A lot of crying.

I wish to elucidate and break down the importance and the reverence behind crying and tears because I know many of you reading this book will go through this.

There is a limiting, large collective belief that crying is weak.

I know that this was a big story that directed a large portion of my childhood and adolescence.

Within this story, we can feel that whenever we are crying, especially if it continues for hours or even days, that we are broken, that we are weak, and that something is wrong.

But let me be very clear with my words, here in this moment: not only is crying not weak, and you are never being too much in your tears,

I would actually classify crying and your tears as a sacred act.

From a physiological perspective, we know that your tears are actually an expression and release of certain toxins, but through an emotional, mental, energetic, and spiritual lens,

when you are crying you are letting go and moving on from energy that is stored and held within you.

When you are crying, you are also allowing your spirit to speak through the physical, 3D form.

In most cases, the spirit is just letting you know that it is there with you, holding you, but it is speaking through the tears themselves.

So next time you get lost within the story that your tears are too much, remind yourself that they are actually helping you be more of what you are.

Let's take a moment now to discuss and break down something I call a trauma complex.

We've spoken in the previous section, through a mental lens, about the roles of inner-child healing, ancestral healing, and a healthy ego.

But I want to put a few points together here through this understanding of what trauma complexes are.

Put simply, a trauma complex is a multifaceted structure of different emotions, thoughts, stories, and beliefs.

To explain this in a simple way, when you have a traumatic event, let's say in your childhood,

let me ask you a question: Were there emotions experienced?

Were there thoughts; were stories created?

And were there beliefs that you then identified and found yourself in because of that event?

This is a trauma complex.

So when we start to release and listen to the 3D that is telling a story, we must understand that these complexes exist and can take time, patience, and compassion to move through.

I have often found myself and people I've been able to support moving through these types of complexes getting stuck in the belief that I'm going around in circles,

or I'm experiencing the same thing, or I am not getting anywhere.

In reality, what's happening is that you're getting to a new side, a new aspect, a new layer of this trauma complex.

So just this understanding alone can help you release a lot of judgment on your own healing journey.

This is how we truly hold space for the body that just wants to speak, let go, help us heal, and express our unique frequency of love.

5
Your Physical Pillar

Our physical pillar is exactly what it sounds like.

It is your beautiful human body or your human, 3D form that holds all of the mental, emotional, and spiritual components that we've been talking about thus far.

It is also the pillar that shares your love frequency here in this dimension.

So with this understanding, we can see the importance of maintaining, supporting, and nourishing this human pillar.

One of my favorite statements to be mindful of around your physical pillar is that the body truly tells the story of your life.

Much like the 3D telling a story in the last chapter, what this shows us is that your physical form is one of the last places in which disease, challenge, trauma, tension, and disconnection from self and your love frequency show up.

So when something appears on the physical layer, it behooves all of us to bring some loving attention to it.

And this is really where the physical pillar comes in. If we can nourish and love our 3D form, then this reverberates through our whole being.

For example, if I'm sitting outside in the sun with my feet on the earth, grounding, rejuvenating through the sun's rays,

which, funnily enough, I'm doing right now, as I write these words,

that choice, through the physical form, impacts me emotionally, mentally, and spiritually, and thus affects my whole holistic being.

This allows me to express my love frequency fully.

But unfortunately, this is not the state, and more specifically, this is not the type of awareness most of us have.

So let's down break why this is and what we can do about it.

In order to support the human pillar and its physical form, we must first realize what's wrong with it.

Or, more accurately, what's wrong with the systems that are leading us into a state of disease: Big Food, Big Pharma, Big Agriculture, and many other systems that play out in the world.

What this environmental ecosystem of bad actors creates is a human that is very sick, very frail, and very dependent on the same systems to continue moving.

As I mentioned in regard to our beliefs, our stories, our trauma, and our emotions,

most of us, including me for very long time, are in a chronic fight-or-flight state.

But in this chapter, we are looking at it through a physical lens; for example,

most of us are drinking toxic water, eating toxic food, breathing shallowly through the chest, not getting enough sleep, and not moving our bodies, and the cycle continues.

This creates a physical pillar that is frail.

This creates a physical form that that can barely stand up, let alone be vibrant and sustain the expression of this beautiful love frequency inside of us that deserves to be shared with the world.

So without writing many novels on what is wrong with the collective systems in the world, what we can focus in on are the solutions.

What we can focus in on is how we take our power back and start to support our physical form, synchronize it with our mind and soul, and thus allow our love frequency to flow.

―――

The easiest way for me to give you some tools, tips, and insights on supporting the physical form without writing ten more novels is to break this down into bite-size action items.

And for this, I will start with "the six foundational principles."

You'll find more information about these foundational principles at the CHEK Institute, based in San Diego California,

which is one of the core certifications, educations, and teachings I've had the privilege of moving through and being taught within.

These six foundation principles are as follows:

Thinking, breathing, eating, drinking, moving, and sleeping.

These foundational principles are your go-to for starting to support the physical pillar and this human form.

If you are stuck, if you're in physical pain, if you're wondering how to nourish yourself today, look through the lens of one of these pillars.

Ask yourself, *How did I sleep last night?*

Ask yourself, *How am I breathing?*

Ask yourself, *What was on my plate?*

What kind of water was I drinking, and have I moved my body today?

From a simplistic view, this is what is needed. Of course, we can always layer on more foundations, more routes to take, but I'm not here to make this complicated for you.

I'm here to give you actionable items to move through.

So I encourage you to continue to ask these questions as you support the physical form to allow your frequency to flow.

And make it simple. Start with a diary where you are ticking off these principles every day, until they become a habit, until they become a routine, until they become a part of your being.

For example, I cannot flow throughout my day without supporting these six areas. As I speak to you now, in this moment, as you read these words,

I'm sitting in the sun to support my movement, about to have lunch to support my nutrition, drinking some filtered water to support my hydration, breathing through my nose to support my breathing, making sure I have a post-lunchtime nap to support my sleep, and, as the last chapter outlines, making sure I'm mindful of the beliefs and stories I'm telling myself.

This is not unique to me.

These steps, these foundations, and these human pillar principles, we can all start to follow, so I leave it to you, dear reader,

What action can you take today?

One of my favorite ways to support the physical and human pillar is through physical touch.

The kinds of physical touch that don't necessarily come from another person.

What I am referring to is the physical touch that comes from yourself.

One of the core inner-child needs that we all deserve to have met is caressing and loving touch.

While this links to our inner-child chapter, what it highlights here, within this physical conversation, is that healthy, loving touch helps us feel safe.

Healthy, loving touch helps us heal, and healthy, loving touch allows the physical human pillar that we are to expand and be strong.

So implement a beautiful self-touching practice into your life to support the physical being, to allow it to express the frequency of love that you deserve.

For me, what this looks like is that whenever I'm practicing yoga, I apply caressing touch to areas of my body, specifically areas that are sore, tight, and stressed,

to let my inner child know that it is safe, that it is loved, and that it is seen.

As an example to highlight this practice, mice studies have shown that litters of mice that were born to a mother that did not lick the skin

and caress the skin grew at different rates than those that did get this loving touch and attention.

So this simple example highlights what you can do for yourself, by stepping in as the mother to reparent and provide yourself the healing touch needed.

This shows the benefit of loving touch on your physical human pillar, not just to meet the needs that deserve to be met

but also to optimize the physicality of your being so your love frequency can expand.

— —

Another powerful, practical tip and tool that we can start to use in optimizing the human, physical pillar of the synchronization and cosmic love antenna process is something another one of my mentors, Paul Chek—the founder of the CHEK Institute, a holistic practitioner, author, and healer—has shared within his teachings that I will now share with you,

and this is a term that he coined, the "pain teacher."

The pain teacher concept, put simply, is starting to see that across all of your holistic being, not just your physical aspects,

pain is an invitation for growth.

And as we start to feel and express pain through the physical pillar, which could come up in reference to any of those six principles,

it is here we have a choice to open ourselves to the guidance that this pain gives us.

For example, if I am starting to feel chronic pain and challenges within my pelvic floor or my hips,

it would be very easy for me to ignore, numb, suppress, and pretend it isn't there.

But if I take on this principle of the pain teacher, with my slight modification of this principle (adding in the breath),

what you can do is start to expand the pain,

to be inquisitive of the pain and reveal the teaching that it provides, thus allowing you to actually move on from the pain, learn the guidance it wishes to impart, and start to illuminate.

Many of us do not do this. And I encourage you, beautiful reader, to start to implement this mindset and physical shift into your daily routine.

Within this physical, human pillar chapter, I want to take a moment now to talk about the challenge of emotional eating.

Throughout this book, I've discussed the role of emotions in bridging the mind, body, and soul.

And this is never more the case than with the addictions, challenges, and pain that come with emotional eating.

A story and example I wish to share to highlight this happened to me last year with a beautiful soul that I was helping.

We were having a discussion around the circumstances of this being's weight gain, and she explained to me, after I asked when she noticed this weight gain starting,

that it was around the death of her child, and during our conversation, I asked her a very important question.

How did this tragic event make her feel?

She replied with one word:

empty.

What this tragic yet beautiful example highlights is how our holistic system of systems works through all of its many different facets. The way that we do one thing is the way that we do all things,

meaning that if we are not meeting our needs emotionally, then those needs will be met mentally, spiritually, or in this case, physically, through the entrance of foods.

But most of us will not be attuned to the underlying challenge here.

In this example, an addiction is formed because the root emotional challenge is not being addressed in the way that it deserves to be addressed.

So within your physical pillar today, where can you observe a physical challenge or a physical opportunity that can be supported by your emotional healing work?

Where can you use this emotional bridge to support your beautiful, physical, human pillar?

—— ——

A powerful practice that you can start today, this week, or this weekend to bring some love back into your human physical pillar and thus

start emitting your love frequency through the body aspect of your holistic being is the practice of yin yoga.

As a yoga teacher, in the last couple of years, I've come to fall in love with this devotional practice, and through the lens of this journey we are taking,

yin yoga as a way in which we approach our movement to support our physical being is a must.

The reason that yin can be so powerful and why I'm adding it into this chapter for you to dive into is that yin yoga isn't like any other standard yoga practice.

What yin prioritizes is slow, steady holds.

In the slow, steady holds, we allow something special to occur. This special trait is allowance.

Of what, you may ask?

Allowance of all that needs to move through you at any given moment.

When you hold a yin yoga pose for two, three, four, five minutes, you're not just hitting the physiological layer of your being,

but you're also allowing any emotional, mental, and spiritual expressions to move up and out of you.

This is where yoga and yin yoga can be powerful.

A fifteen-, twenty-, or thirty-minute practice every other day can allow you to move through the 3D telling a story, address your inner child, and break your ancestral chains while also improving your physical posture, aligning your meridians, chakras, and energy centers, and leaving you feeling great.

This practice fits perfectly into our cosmic love antenna conversation because it works across not just your body

But, as stated, your mind and spirit too.

So go out and take advantage of this beautiful process.

Within your human pillar, it's very important to understand that just because the symptoms are physical,

that doesn't mean the root problem or the root challenge is also physical.

What do I mean by this?

Well, throughout this chapter, we've discussed ways in which you can support your physical human pillar, and one of those ways, was the benefit of your six foundational principles.

Your thinking, your breathing, your eating, your drinking, your moving, and your sleeping.

Let me take one of these as a point to make here: your eating. And let's say that you fall into the camp that, unfortunately, most of us do,

where you have challenges, gut aches, gut dysbiosis, leaky gut, and gut illness.

We could look at this purely through a physical lens, looking at what you're feeding your body, what toxins you're exposed to, and what rest you're giving that gut; all are important.

What we could also do, and what I have often found, is that the more long-term solution to a physical symptom is to look at the emotional root (like the example with the lady above).

Now we again bring in the emotional bridge within your mind, body, and soul,

synchronizing this time through the physical layer.

A gut challenge, from an energetic and emotional viewpoint, can often be traced back to, one, your boundaries and personal power being taken away,

And two, your inner-child wounds, inner challenges, and inner-child stress.

If you experienced rejection or abandonment as a child and this created feelings of unworthiness, guilt, shame, and anger, and they were not acknowledged and released,

then these emotions, these stories, these beliefs are being stored.

Where are they being stored?

In the gut, the solar plexus, and the stomach, causing stress.

And how do you think this stress shows itself through the physical form?

Well, one of the ways is through that gut distress, that leaky gut, and those gut aches.

So I show this example to help you see that just because we have a physical symptom and a physical challenge, that doesn't mean we have to handle it through a physical lens.

And this should empower you, beautiful reader, and help you see that there is always a way through, even if it doesn't seem obvious.

Another reason that it is so imperative for you, the beautiful reader, to optimize and synchronize your body overall

(but specifically the human pillar that we speak about in this chapter) is because of the two kinds of energy systems that you run on.

What I mean by this is that most of us have heard of our internal energy system.

This is the cellular, mitochondrial energy system that is based on external input:

the food, air, and sunlight that we take in, which the cells then utilize to create and produce cellular energy.

What a lot of us overlook is the deep internal energy that is created often in unison with spiritual connection, that is outside of this mitochondrial system.

More important, this spiritual, soulful energy is created by our spirit when we are aligned with our purpose, our passions, and our love frequency.

These two energy systems interact with each other.

The external dependent, cellular system and the deep internal, soulful, spiritual system interact.

What is the medium that they interact through?

Your physical human pillar.

So when we are adding inputs such as food, proper hydration, proper breathing, proper movement, and proper sleeping actions,

we allow for the external dependent system to produce the energy that we need, and then the expression of our soulful, loving energy can be optimized.

While these systems can act on their own, they are enhanced when approached together.

So feel into and acknowledge them as you step forward within your love frequency and start to accept where one system needs more attention

and where the other can be embodied to continue your journey.

A very important point to make within this focus on the physical body is the role of feeling and sensing through the physical, 3D form.

Throughout this section of the book, we've talked about prioritizing and healing and releasing a lot of the emotion, tension, and pain that is being held in the body.

However, what I want to focus on now is what starts to happen once we remove these layers of illusion, once we remove these pains and challenges,

we switch our ability to feel the world outside of us back on.

And this is important for many reasons, but the reason I want to draw your attention to in this moment is that when we drop into the body and feel what is being felt or sensed through our skin,

when we feel what is moving through us in any given moment, we tap into the only moment that matters, the present.

In this present moment, it is through the physical, 3D form that we are able to channel our spirit, our essence, or, in the context of this beautiful book,

our love frequency.

So I share this with you, beautiful reader, to underline the importance of using your body to feel in any given moment.

I've spoken about something else many times thus far: the overemphasis, in this reality, on just using the thinking mind.

We're not here to push the mind away, but we are here to add an end to this one sided conversation of the mind being our only point of reference,

and that end is accomplished by feeling and sensing through the physical body.

Prioritize this today and take note of what comes up.

—— ——

Once you start to prioritize your human, physical pillar, you must understand what your true base state is.

What do I mean by this?

Well, if you were to look at a lot of the collective institutions out there in the world, such as Big Medicine, Big Food, Big Pharma, and Big "insert industrialized power here,"

it would be easy to see and think that your base state is one of disease, challenge, pain, sickness, tiredness, etc.

But in my own personal healing journey

and for many beautiful souls that I have been able to help, the true base state is one of abundance.

Your true base state is one of balance, homeostasis, and vitality.

If you find yourself in a state that is not this—a state of disease, a state of pain, a state of challenge, a state of imbalance in any way—

then you must remind yourself that if you are to truly use your physical body, activating your cosmic love antenna and thus your love frequency,

that your base state is one of homeostasis, health, and beautiful balance.

Just this mindset shift alone can change how you show up and see the larger world.

— —

I want to take a moment to highlight something very significant here as we finish this chapter,

and it is the role of the physical body in helping you experience your emotional purpose.

What do I mean by that?

It is my belief,

that we are spiritual beings having physical human experiences

here on the 3D earth, experiencing all of its lessons through the physical body,

through emotional experiences.

Let me ask you a question. When you experience emotions,

does it feel objectively neutral, or do you feel certain sensations, certain tensions, certain openings, certain expansions?

This is what I mean.

Your physical body is the instrument with which you open yourself up to the emotional experiences of life

that this spiritual being is here and meant to experience.

So when we deny our emotional sensitivities through the human, physical, 3D pillar,

we also deny our biggest purpose for being here in this incarnation.

I cannot emphasize this enough.

So when we start to optimize and heal the physical body, of course we become more sensitive because sensitivity is one of the reasons we are here on this earth in this beautiful moment in time.

6
Chakra Gateways

ne of my intentions in writing this book for you, dear reader, is to simplify many overwhelming themes, topics, and self-healing tools out there today

so your love frequency can be emitted strongly and brightly.

One of said topics is your beautiful chakra system.

These energy portals within your mental, emotional, spiritual, and, in this chapter, physical healing are very important.

But out there in the collective understanding, there are just as many views and understandings as there are practitioners teaching about these beautiful energy portals.

So I say this to encourage you to feel these words, feel a frequency behind them as I explain their importance not just in your mind, body, and soul synchronization

but in what you will inevitably start to emit through your love frequency.

Your energy portals, your chakras, are the gateway to your mind, body, and soul synchronization.

They're also the way in which we can check in with ourselves on a daily basis to see how our love frequency is being emitted or why it is not.

This is because your energy centers are a powerful storehouse of life-force energy,

and this energy information moves across your mental, emotional, physical, and spiritual being.

So let's dive deeper into their power and their relationship to your cosmic love antenna.

Your chakra gateways should be seen as a daily space of introspection.

What I mean by this is that each of the main chakra portals—your root, your sacral, your solar plexus, your heart, your throat, your third eye, and your crown—

can act as a check-in point throughout your day to see what needs to be cleared and or opened.

One of the best representations of these energy centers is a lotus flower that is constantly opening and closing throughout your day based on the interactions that you have.

Because we're speaking about these energy centers within the body section, or the physical being section, of this journey,

these lotus flowers are important in that they help us to connect any feelings, sensations, or pain not just to an area of the 3D body

but also to a corresponding energy center.

For example, a lot of my challenges with my stomach and gut have also been related to suppressing and ignoring the anger flowing through me.

So how this often expresses itself through the physical being is stomach upset, stomach sinking, stomach challenges and pain.

This is just one nuanced example, but you can learn to tune into how your physical being speaks to you through these energy centers with nuanced guidance,

and much like the 3D telling a story, your energy centers keep track.

So you can see, feel, release, and come back to physical balance.

This is their power, and this is how we start to use them to bring homeostasis back to the human pillar.

While these chakra gateways can be seen through the mental lens and the spiritual, soulful lens

in this physical chapter, I ask you purely to start from here.

You can begin by noticing the sensations throughout your body.

One of the best ways we can do this is start keeping what I call an "emotional log" or an "energetic log."

This entails noticing throughout your day all the different interactions you have with friends, family members, and lovers, and noticing how your body responds to these interactions.

For example, after you speak to your father, do you notice anger moving through you and sensations in the solar plexus or stomach region?

When you get off the phone with your mom, do you feel your throat start to close, with your throat starting to have a tingle in it and that throat chakra activating?

When you finish speaking in front of your colleagues at work, do you notice your forehead and third eye starting to tingle?

Do you feel sensations across that forehead area at the same moment in time?

All of these are examples of how your beautiful energy centers and chakra portals are speaking to you through the physical body, and they're not speaking to be ignored.

While they don't judge, they are offering guidance for you to lean into.

So use this simple tool and simple act to start opening and coming back to a deeper relationship with these gateways.

And what you'll notice is that your beautiful sensitivities will start to increase not just through the physical body,

but they'll start to go deeper mentally, emotionally, and ultimately spiritually, and every single step of the way, your chakra portals will guide you.

Today, start with just one step.

One very important reason that these chakra portals are pivotal in synchronizing the physical as a part of your cosmic love antenna

Is that they help us come back to an internal foundation.

What is this internal foundation?

Well, if you look at the chakra system overall, the first chakra is your root.

And this root chakra has the function of helping you come back to an internal sense of safety, security, and support.

In the world that we live in, there are many beautiful humans, myself included, walking around unable to capture these very three pivotal internal sensations.

Let me ask you, the beautiful reader, how often do you feel safe in your body?

How often do you feel secure in your body?

How often do you feel supported in your body?

Whether it's due to trauma,

whether it's due to external global events,

like COVID-19, wars, and recessions,

whether it's due to a toxic environment of food, chemicals, and substances,

we live in a collective ecosystem that leaves the individual in a hypervigilant, fight-or-flight, stressed-out state.

So it is no wonder that we do not feel these internal feelings of safety, security, and support, because we're always looking outside of ourselves for the thing that wants to come get us.

So it is in this very understanding that we can see the importance of these chakra gateways.

Because if we can come back into this connection and find our own internal sense of safety, security, and support through the root chakra

and the chakra system as a whole, then suddenly we are not

dependent on a food, a lover, or a substance to get lost in and find these feelings externally.

One of the most common questions I get when working with lovely souls in the chakra gateways paradigm to help them connect their love frequency

is, *What do we do once an emotion comes up?*

If we're looking to connect back into the physical human pillar, and we are using these chakra gateways within this exploration,

we're probably noticing that some emotions are moving through us

whether they be anger, sadness, grief, shame, guilt, etc.

What do we do when they arise?

Or, put simply, we must ask the question in this moment once more,

What is an emotion, and what characteristics does it hold?

Is an emotion innately positive?

Is an emotion innately negative?

I would first answer this question with "neither." An emotion, put simply, is energy.

Put in a more complex way, it is energy in motion.

So when an emotion comes up, either when doing chakra work or any kind of physical healing,

what we must do is get out of its way.

Allow that emotion to lean into what it's meant to do.

Move.

For many of us, this might look like actually physically moving through exercise, dancing, walking, running, boxing, etc.

This might look like using your beautiful words and voice to channel this emotion through the throat chakra.

This might look like writing, journaling, getting it out through the written word.

This might look like dropping into meditation and allowing other states of energetic release to occur,

such as somatic shaking or crying.

The point here is when the emotional bridge of the physical body arises, we must lean in, and we must allow the emotion to channel itself through us.

And I would not be surprised if in this very act, unintentionally at first, you opened up more of the channel for your powerful love frequency to be expressed and ignited.

Within this chakra gateways chapter, now I wish to share a term and a series of tips and tools you can use to move through a lot of the emotions and beliefs and stories being stored in the body, which are restricting your love frequency.

This is a term I coined *the sacral tree*, and it refers to not just your sacral chakra but all of the activities and branches that stem from the sacral foundation.

Your sacral chakra is your creation.

And in many ways, this creation energy is connected to your divinity, which we'll talk about in the next chapters.

But for now, I want you to hold this image of the tree and hold the sacral chakra as the roots or the trunk of the tree itself.

Then, as we branch upward toward the leaves and the larger branches, these represent all of the different ways we can start to open our sacral and heal.

These branches represent your connection to childlike play.

These branches represent sexual pleasure with yourself or another.

These branches represent the creative act of expression, be it dancing, singing, or moving.

These sacral branches are also connected to your creation of money and finances and business and entrepreneurial activities.

All of these branches come back to your sacral base.

So the point is that all of these different activities can open up your creation energy and thus heal this center.

So ask yourself today, where can you apply the sacral tree to bring balance, harmony, and ultimately love to this area of your being?

―――

A beautiful event to watch out for once you start to open up your chakra gateways within your physical being on this road back to your love frequency is the occurrence and the awakening of your spiritual senses.

I wish to express these within this chapter, through your physical body, to show you the mystical power that is awaiting you.

As I've spoken about earlier, we aren't just thinking beings.

We are thinking, feeling, intuiting, and sensing beings.

One of the parameters in which consciousness moves through us is not just our senses but our spiritual senses.

These are often referred to as your *clair* senses.

I wish to mention them here because it is often the awakening and the activation of your chakra centers that allows these *clair* senses to open.

Your *clair* senses are your clairvoyance, your clairsentience, your clairaudience, your clairalience, and your clairgustance.

Put simply, this is seeing, feeling, hearing, tasting, and smelling, but these are the spiritual versions of them.

So I share these for you to look out for once you start feeling into your chakra portals through your physical body.

Because most people already have one of these senses activated.

You might be seeing beyond your physical vision.

You might be feeling guides along your skin.

You might be tasting things that are not there, smelling things that are not physically there, or even hearing that which is beyond this 3D realm.

One of the ways this deepens is through the opening of your third eye, through the opening of your heart chakra, and through the opening of your crown.

So if this is you, I encourage you to lean in, seek support, and seek guidance

but know that this, in my opinion, is a very healthy step on your path back to your love frequency.

I want to take this opportunity as we wrap up this chapter and section of the journey to make a very important connection for you.

Within this chakra chapter, I want to emphasize the holistic nature of these energetic portals and gateways,

specifically between the physical body, your hormones, and your mental, emotional, and spiritual nature.

There is a reason that most if not all of the chakra gateways are connected to a hormonal gland or center.

The sacral and the root are connected to your adrenal glands,

your heart is connected to your thymus,

your throat is connected to your thyroid,

and your third eye and crown are connected to your pineal and pituitary glands.

This is not a coincidence.

This is because your chakra gateways and overall system are the bridge that the hormones run across.

What am I saying here?

What I'm getting at, beautiful reader, is that if you are having hormonal challenges such as hyper- or hypothyroidism or adrenal fatigue

and you're looking to go a bit deeper and activate your cosmic love antenna and thus your love frequency, moving through your hormonal challenges will be a symptom of this work.

Now, of course, I cannot make any medical claims; that would not be ethically correct for me.

But what I can say from my own experience is that if you're looking to express your love frequency,

and you also have these hormonal obstacles in your way, I give you so much love in knowing that these two areas of interest hold a one in the same solution.

Meaning, by bringing loving attention and awareness to your chakra gateways, due to the link they have via the hormonal bridge, you now open up space for deeper healing across your body, mind, and spirit.

Part 3
Soul

7
The Longest Road of All

ur spirit and soul are waiting to be embodied and acknowledged.

It's very important to understand that your spirit and soul are made of this love frequency that we have been talking about for this entire journey together.

So the degree to which you accept and embrace your spiritual, soulful essence

is the degree to which you start to emit this love frequency that I've spoken about in depth throughout this journey thus far.

But I want to share here a part of my experience that I've come to understand regarding my spirit and soul.

And this also connects to this chapter as a whole in why, exactly, it can be so hard to take the journey from the head to the heart.

My spirit and my soul have been around for many incarnations, and there is a high chance, if you're moving through this experience with me,

that your soul has also.

With this understanding, we can then take the next progression to see that my soul and your soul

have most likely not just been around many times here on this earth but have also been around many times in this galactic environment and universe.

Through my own exploration of this, I've come to remember and realize that there is deep galactic and celestial trauma in my soul and most likely in yours. (I know, going super *woo*; stick with me!)

This I would count as *starseed trauma* or *starseed pain*, and much like the emotional, mental, and physical trauma,

this spiritual and soulful starseed trauma must be accepted, understood, and moved through the same way. This is where I often find challenges and obstacles between the head and the heart in myself and in people that have come to see me.

A starseed put simply is a soul who has spent many lifetimes and much of its existence outside of this earthly planet.

It is the starseed, celestial and galactic trauma from the Orion wars, from Syrian wars, from many other galactic and universal painful experiences that keep us traumatized.

So with this story and this preface,

let us go into the next chapters understanding that our soul and our spirit wish to be seen in all of their light and shadows, just as much as our physical, mental, and emotional bodies do.

―――

Now it's time to take a step even deeper, to take your journey of mind-body-soul synchronizing and the expansion of your love frequency into the soulful, spiritual depths.

Our first stop within this world is bringing loving observation to the longest path you'll ever take.

And this is from your head to your heart.

We live in a world where it is so easy for us to feel that the only way to interact with reality is through our minds.

And as we discussed in the mind chapters and also regarding the physical pillar, this can be a problem because our mind isn't in that beautiful garden state.

It isn't trauma-free, pain-free, or distortion-free.

So you can see how this creates a kind of human that is interacting with the world outside of itself from a state of challenge.

So this path that we now take into the heart gives us an option.

This path into the heart lets us awaken.

And this path into the heart lets us move forward into our own internal frequency and a space of love, but let's start to dissect why this is so important and why this is the first section of the soul-synchronizing arena.

—

I grew up within an education system that not only taught me what to think, not how to think,

but that also never even touched on topics such as intuition, mysticism, and spirituality,

let alone the spirit and the soul.

And while I do try to hold compassion for the education system that many of us grew up in,

I do wish to highlight a big lack of expression and a very limited way of interacting with the world.

I was unaware of my ability to see the world through my heart.

I was unaware of my ability to interact with others from a space of love.

And this is troublesome; this is a problem. Because, again, as we discussed in our path through the mind, our brains, our minds, are easily programmable, and most of us are not programming them in an expansive way.

So the reason that this is the longest path you'll ever take is that we have to move through a lot of these challenges and obstacles.

But I encourage you, beautiful reader, to spend a bit more time in this heart, and if you followed all of the chapters up to this point,

from your mind to your body to the soulful words you're now reading,

you're almost ready to start not just experiencing the world through this heart space

but remembering your unique love frequency, which will do most of this work for you.

For it is the frequency that is in this heart; it is the frequency of your love that you can now use outside of your mind,

outside of your thinking ego, to communicate, to feel, and to intuitively sense other options.

Whether these other options concern your health,

your relationships, or your life path, passions, and purpose,

all of this applies to your heart, to your love and your unique frequency.

Let's speak for a moment, here on our journey from the head to the heart, about all things karma.

One of the reasons why this journey from the head to the heart is so long is because of this one concept: karma.

A lot of the challenges that arise from it involve many misunderstandings.

In my perspective, karma, put simply, is balanced or unbalanced energy, balanced or unbalanced choices.

I either make a choice from love, unity, and connection, and this brings balanced karma,

or I make a choice from fear, separation, and illusion,

and this leaves unbalanced karma.

This accrues over many lifetimes in our different incarnations.

And the reason that this is important to understand is that it is often what is being triggered and challenged within our mind, within our body, and through our spirit and soul as we journey back to our sacred love frequency.

So within any given moment, if you can make a choice from love, unity, and connection

and be mindful of the karma that is triggered, you can seek to resolve said karma and go deeper into oneself.

What is in this space of deepness?

Well, in most cases, this is your love frequency.

Take away any other misunderstandings around what karma is and apply this teaching, apply this education, because I've found, both in my own life and in those of the people I've been able to support,

that this understanding of karma makes the journey from the head to the heart a lot more authentic and transformational.

—   —

Another big indicator and root cause of why the road from the head to the heart in your spiritual development is so long

is contained in two words:

religious trauma.

While I could write a whole separate novel—and who knows, this might be in my future—

what I want to help you, the lovely reader, understand in this moment is that most of us,

myself included, have experienced some kind of religious separation or trauma event, either in this life or down our ancestral line,

and I don't say this to offend. I don't say this to scare; I don't even say this to throw any kind of hate or judgment on the religions and their beautiful communities that currently exist.

It is my belief and perspective that there are beautiful, loving, compassionate, mystical foundations in all of the world's religions.

Unfortunately, there are a lot of manmade layers on top of each and every one of them that cause a lot of pain,

that have caused a lot of tension, separation, and trauma.

I bring this up in this chapter to help you illuminate why, exactly, this journey from the head to the heart can be so challenging, because most of us, again,

either in this lifetime or the lifetimes that we exist within, have been taught through this religious dogma that we are separate from our power.

We are separate from God, and we are separate from our loving frequency.

If this is a belief that we hold either consciously or unconsciously, you can see how we would cut ourselves off from the revelation of what the truth actually is.

And that truth, dear soul, is that God was never outside of you.

Your divinity is inextricably linked to the love frequency that expands through your cosmic love antenna.

Lets keep this journey from the head to the heart flowing and talk about how often we get stuck in the belief that this is our first time taking this journey.

And for a small percentage of us, this may be true.

However, in my experience, the real reality is that most of us have done this before.

What do I mean by this?

What I mean by this, as alluded to above, is that the beautiful soul and spirit that are part of your love frequency, which I'm here to help you embody and emit,

have had, in most instances, many lives, many experiences, many stories that they have been a part of

and that they have told.

So, dear reader, what I would encourage you to do is to open your heart to this understanding.

And please do not take my word for this.

I'd encourage you to seek out a past-life regression practitioner or a hypnotherapist.

Either of these practitioners can support you in remembering this journey that you've taken.

And the reason this is powerful is that the answers truly lie within you.

Most of us are not getting these answers because we're not asking the right questions.

Our belief systems, which are inherently closed, keep us in a paradigm without us knowing what is outside of it.

So if you're stuck in the mind and unable to drop into your heart, your spirit, your soul, and your love frequency,

your solutions may exist in the lives that you've lived already.

But the question is, do you feel confident enough, courageous enough, to dive into them?

―― ―

What I would love to do now is to give you another simple understanding of exactly why this road from the head to the heart can be so difficult for many.

And I'm going to explain this through a healing modality that I use with clients and beautiful souls who come to see me.

This is using your dreams at night to start to heal.

Your dreams at night are a very powerful area of your consciousness that you can farm and mine for deeper stages of healing.

And when you're looking to emit your love frequency, your dream world and specifically the nightmares that you often have are a good example of this.

Without getting into a whole dream lecture here to explain nightmares,

very simply, in most cases a nightmare is a reflection of your shadow.

And your shadow is the complex of suppressed pieces of yourself that you have either consciously or, in most cases, unconsciously stored.

When we start to embrace and heal through nightmares, we start to heal and integrate our shadows.

Once we start to heal and integrate our shadows through our nightmares, what this starts to do is to make this journey from the head to the heart a lot simpler.

This is because we are no longer triggered by so many of the repressed aspects of self in our external world.

As we all know very well, it is much easier for us to project our pain than to deal with it.

And our nightmares at night become an opportunity to deal with this pain, integrate our shadows back into the light, and take a further step from the head to the heart.

I highly recommend working with your nightmares, either with myself (please see the details at the end of the book) or with any kind of coach, clinician, or psychologist that can help you analyze and dive deeper into your dreams and nightmare world.

—-— —-—

The next powerful tool I wish to share with you is what I describe as your *totem animals*.

In many shamanic practices and worldviews, totem animals are well-known.

Put simply for the sake of this journey, a totem animal is a mystical and spiritual representation of a real-world animal entity.

These totem animals come with guidance, symbology, and meaning to help you get further down your path.

Within the context of this book, with the goals of activating your cosmic love antenna and your love frequency and synchronizing your mind, body, and soul,

these totem animals can be just the guidance we need when we get stuck on the road from the head to the heart.

What does this look like, however, and how can we lean in to these beautiful messages?

Well, one of the ways that I love to connect to them is through a simple meditation.

If you're getting stuck in your head and still finding it hard to open up the mystical space that is your heart center,

I encourage you to drop into a meditation and either call to a totem animal that you've already connected to

or set the intention to connect to a brand-new totem animal and then allow its presence to be made manifest to you.

It could appear as a vision,

it could appear as a sensation,

it could appear as a smell,

or it could appear as a sound.

The important thing to acknowledge here is to allow yourself to receive them.

Allow yourself to be with them in whatever way they decide to appear.

I'd recommend writing down how this experience impacted you and then working with someone, either a coach, a practitioner, a mentor, or a guide, to help you go deeper into the gift they gave you.

This wisdom could also be gathered from your own higher self and your own intuition,

but sometimes it's best to reflect it off of someone that has experience with these kinds of animals.

The summary here, though, is not to be afraid to call to these beautiful entities in the mystical world,

because they could be just what you need to overcome the challenge that is blocking your expression back into the heart space.

— —

Another big obstacle on the road from the head to the heart that I've noticed in a lot of clients and beautiful souls in general that I've encountered in my world

is the illusion that we are moving backward, especially after our challenges.

Throughout this journey that we've taken together, I've mentioned multiple times

that we are frequency, or we are energy.

And if we are energy at a very fundamental level, then we have to ask ourselves, *What is the nature of energy?*

Through the quantum lens I predominantly live in,

we understand that energy is neither created or destroyed but rather is either moving or transforming into something else.

And when I say moving, I mean moving forward.

So with this perspective, we can understand that in the context of this chapter, when we are moving along our journey from the head to the heart and we get stuck in the illusion that we are moving backward, through old patterns of the same resonance,

then it is here we can remind ourselves that we are not moving backward, because it is energetically and fundamentally not doable.

What does occur, however, is that this feeling of moving backward is, in reality,

a stepping-forward from a space of decompression rather than from a space of expansion.

We always have a choice in the steps that we take.

However, most of us are taking steps forward from a space of fear, illusion, and separation.

This is why we can feel like we're moving backward, but instead, what is happening is that we're moving forward in a decompressed or "small" state.

So the lesson and the education here is to catch yourself next time you feel like you're moving backward and ask, *Why do I feel small?*

Why do I feel separate?

Why do I feel fearful?

And then test this and ask, *Can I make a different choice, or is there something I can let go of?*

At this point in our beautiful journey together, you must understand that your heart is not just the space in which you feel certain emotions, sadness, grief, and different layers of love,

but it is also the seat of your soul.

It has a space in which your spirit and soul spends most of their time.

So when we interact and view the world through our hearts, when we start to define our love frequencies, we are truly letting the spiritual side of ourselves through,

and if we can do this more and more,

we start to interact with all of the people, places, and things that we love through the spiritual lens

rather than just our mental, physical, or emotional way of being.

This brings a holistic approach to the way in which we flow through the world.

And all of this starts in the heart.

But I'll end this chapter by adding some compassion and letting you know that if you're having trouble with this,

if you're having challenges with this soulful and spiritual understanding, if this is still bringing up tension and resistance, then there is work to be done here,

and I would encourage you to go back and look over the physical being and the mental being that you are,

now with this deeper understanding, as stated above.

It may hit you differently and allow you to work through this very resistance and confusion.

The chapters previously broke down each of the steps for this very reason, to help you work up to this.

And if you're having trouble on this longest of roads, most of the time, this is because there is a challenge within the physical

or the mental that has yet to be integrated.

So have grace and patience and move through these,

and I promise you, the path will start to reveal itself.

8
Heart-Space Portal

Now that we've taken this long journey from the head to the heart, what exactly is our destination in this heart space?

Is this heart portal just a chakra?

Is it just a place where we feel deep emotions of love, sadness, grief, melancholy, longing, and desire?

Or is it something more?

Is your heart-space portal actually an opening and a gateway to this love frequency we've been talking about for this entire expedition?

This, of course, is a hypothetical question. Because your heart-space portal is exactly this:

it is the space and place from which your love frequency is emitted.

It is the gateway to your multidimensional being. It is the space in which you start to express your uniqueness to the world.

And it is really why we have been doing this whole mind-body-soul synchronization, to allow this frequency to come forth from this heart-space portal.

We know now, through the work that's been done at places like the HeartMath Institute, that your heart has an electromagnetic frequency that can be measured.

We know that you can walk into a room in any setting and pick up on the vibe.

What are you picking up on?

Well, in many situations, you're picking up on the frequencies of the people that inhabit that same location.

This is your heart-space portal.

And this is where we want to start spending more of our time.

All the work that we've been doing can help us open this place, but now we must start making the choice to actively spend more time here.

What does this look like?

When we actively decide to spend time in our heart-space portal, we make choices from a place of love rather than a place of fear, worry, anxiety, tension, or separation.

One of my favorite ways to step through or into this love is to ask the question, *What does it look like to embody love?*

What would it look like if I took my next step from a place of love, from a place of connection, from place of unity?

How would love act, moving through the fear, worry, and anxiety that's coming up?

This is a question and a stepping-forward that we can use in all directions of our life, across our business, our relationships, and our health choices.

When we move forward with love, we move from this heart-space portal.

But this is even more significant than all of the above.

Because when we're moving from love, what are we doing?

This is the soul section of this book.

As I stated in a previous reflection, your spirit and soul live in this heart space.

So when you are making a choice and moving forward with love, you're also moving forward from that spiritual being that you are.

And this starts to become profound because you're moving forward from the big self rather than the small self.

What does this mean?

This means that when we step forward with love, from the heart, from our soul, from our spirit,

we are stepping forward from the larger part of what we are.

That larger part is all the sections of us that are connected to the whole.

The sections of us that are connected to our deepest power, our deepest potential, our deepest possibilities.

When we make a choice from love through our heart-space portal, we're channeling the present moment's potential into action.

And this is not just any kind of action; this is inspired action.

This is what manifestation and creation energy is made of.

So as you can see now, with this heart-space portal, your love choice and moving through this energy starts to create a very different reality.

In contrast with choices made from the ego and the mind, which are often encumbered by your inner-child trauma, your ancestral wounds, and your limiting beliefs, these choices are made from a very different consciousness.

So that is really what we're saying here.

You are now deciding to make decisions and take actions from a consciousness that is built on love rather than pain, trauma, separation, and disconnection.

And when you ask me if this is a world I want to live in,

where everyone is stepping forward with this kind of frequency and acting from this space of love rather than from a place of tension and trauma,

I know where I land and what my answer will be.

—   —

Within our heart-space portal, as we unlock the deeper layers of this powerful, mystical heart on the road back to our love frequency,

something that is very deep and profound to understand is the role of our shadows along this healing journey.

Throughout this journey, I've discussed trauma and healing in many different ways.

And right now, through the heart-space portal context, I want to discuss shadow work and what the shadows in this healing modality bring us once we start to view them through the lens of the heart.

When we illuminate, heal, and transmute the shadows that come up along our spiritual, mental, and physical synchronization on the road to our cosmic love antenna's activation,

we start to see that our shadows come with messages, insights, and gifts to bring us deeper into ourselves.

If we can acknowledge this and, most important, accept and embrace it,

then our journey is accelerated.

For just like our light brings value,

our shadows bring just as much when we alchemize these same beautiful dark aspects, which have been pushed into the corners of our being for many different unconscious reasons.

We gain back more of ourselves, and this is truly enlightening.

Let's pause to quickly define what a *channel* is.

I've referred to channeling multiple times throughout this adventure thus far,

and some of you might be relatively new to this word and its connection to who you are.

In my opinion, there are many misconceptions when it comes to channeling.

I know that in my own story, when I first came across the idea of channeling, I thought it was only for the specifically gifted people that could connect to guides, channeling with their eyes rolling back into their into their heads and speaking in tongues.

And funnily enough, while this can be a component of channeling,

this is not the deepest form of what a channel is and what you are.

Taught simply, a channel is what you were born to be.

A channel is you opening up your divine connection to the deeper frequencies of what you are.

What is an example of this frequency?

This is the love frequency we have discussed.

What do your mind, body, and emotions represent within this channel?

This is your cosmic love antenna.

So, in many ways, we have spoken in-depth about being a channel already,

but within this point and these paragraphs, I want to quickly address the limiting belief that you are not worthy of this gift.

Beautiful reader and dear soul, to channel more of yourself is your birthright.

To be a divine channel, you never needed to do or gain anything.

It was a part of your soul's mission here on this earth.

Yes, the kind of channeling and final expression of it may look different for each and every one of us.

But your channel is innate. The question is,

Will you accept it?

Once we start going deeper into our heart-space portal, we start to understand the channel of love that has been within us this entire time,

what it feels like, and how it expresses itself through us in unique ways.

This is pivotal in understanding your cosmic love antenna and the love frequency we wish to emit.

Because how we start to emit our love frequency is by channeling it through ourselves, embodying it in our 3D forms and sharing it with the external world.

Once this begins, we will notice where we are most likely channeling this frequency and where we are not.

This will be in our relationships.

This is a very significant piece of understanding because if we can comprehend that our love frequency starts to channel in relationship with another,

then we can start to notice something very special.

When we channel our love in the direction of a friend, a family member, or an intimate partner, we notice that we aren't just pouring our love into them.

That love often comes back, boomerangs back into our heart space,

either as a beautiful, expansive feeling or even as a painful feeling that needs more understanding and introspection.

In either situation, the channeling of our love is a two-way street.

We are never just channeling for ourselves.

We're always channeling for the other party in the relationship, back and forth.

If we can allow ourselves to hone this, then it starts to become a superpower and an opportunity for us to learn in every relationship purely through expressing our love frequency from one heart to another.

At the time of writing this book, I have had the divine pleasure of experiencing this actively over the last few years, not only in my personal and work life but also at a very in-depth level through a profound spiritual mystery school taught by the embodied Ascended Master Channel, spiritual teacher, and counsellor In'easa Ishtar.

If this kind of spiritual work specifically calls to you, I encourage you to seek out deeper guidance within this school and from this amazing woman.

As I start to write these next words, I get excited because helpful tool that I now want to address in regard to your heart-space portal have to do with your dreaming world.

When I speak about dreams, there is so much I can share with you, and who knows, in the future,

that may be the topic and the foundation of my next set of writings.

But for the purpose of this chapter, on the topic of your heart-space portal, I want to implore and encourage you to look into your dreams at night.

Your dreamscape, from my experience and perspective, plays two very important roles.

Role one is to foster loving communication between your unconscious and conscious mind to help you with challenges in your waking state.

This communication often occurs through symbology in the dreams themselves.

Role two of your dreams, and this is where your heart-space portal comes in,

is to be a playground where your soulful or spiritual body can run wild.

One of my favorite references to the dreamscape is that the only difference between the waking world and the dreamworld is that in the dreaming world, we don't doubt ourselves,

and this could not be truer.

When it comes to the spiritual nature of our dreamscape, it is in our dreams that we have access to our spiritual abilities, our spiritual insights, our spiritual downloads, and, in reference to your heart-space portal, a deeper remembering of what your love frequency actually is.

This is due to the releasing of the shackles of fear, doubt, limitation and separation, often found in our waking consciousness.

So while we await another book for me to dive deeply into all things dreams,

I would for now honor what your dreams are and get excited about their ability to open you up.

And I would begin with starting a dream journal,

writing down anything that occurs during your dreams at night and then starting to watch and observe how your dreams start to unfold.

This is step one, a beautiful unfolding.

―――

A term that I want to introduce you to now to is *heart compass*.

Your heart compass is a powerful inner awareness that you can learn to come back to.

Once you dive deeper into your heart-space portal through the activation of your cosmic love antenna and the emission of your love frequency, as we've been talking about throughout this adventure,

one of the outputs of the whole process is your heart compass.

Your heart compass is the powerful way in which you're now able to make choices along your soul's journey.

Each and every one of us, in most instances, have two choices we can make.

Whether it be through our business or relationships or along our health journey,

we are either making a choice from our heads, as referred to in the mind chapters,

or we're making a choice from our hearts.

When we make a choice from our heads, it often leaves us swimming upstream.

It might give us short-term gain, but eventually it leaves us pushing against resistance, pushing against the flow of our life.

When we make a choice with our hearts, when we use our heart compasses to direct us, we float down the stream.

This does not mean there will not be challenges or that we will not move over any rocks and obstacles.

But what it does mean is that when we do hit those obstacles and challenges, we feel as if we are supported; we feel as if we are guided; we feel as if we can handle whatever the challenge is.

And this is the power of your heart compass.

Once this muscle starts to build through your heart portal, you can now use this compass in any situation in which you want to know the best choice to make.

Often, your heart compass speaks through your chest, through feelings and sensations, through an expansive feeling or a light feeling or an open feeling.

As these sensations start to expand, your heart compass does also.

And this, beautiful reader, is another muscle connected to your love frequency that will allow you to take further steps towards your bright, unique expression.

Once you've spent enough time in your heart-space portal and you start to feel your love frequency being expressed through yourself,

what you will notice is that your sensitivities, feelings, and emotions will become more attuned—

and I want to make a distinction here. When I say *more attuned* or *heightened*, I do not mean *overwhelming*.

A limiting belief I have referenced multiple times is that that being sensitive or emotional or too much in your feeling is a weakness;

if anything, it is your superpower.

And once we unlock our heart-space portal and our love frequency, we are more sensitive and emotional to the world around us.

But I share this here, in this moment, to help you acknowledge that when you are being your emotional, feeling, and sensitive self,

your authenticity attracts others toward you.

It is through this sensitive, emotional, authentic state that you become beautifully real and magnetize all those outside of you.

I highlight this because I acknowledge that many of you reading this may have the intention of bringing in a beautiful, intimate partner or relationship.

And I wish to affirm for you now, in this moment, that all of this love-frequency work through your sensitivities, feelings, and emotions, in this context, will help you do this.

Because it is through your raw, sensitive expression that people are able to acknowledge and feel safe enough to be themselves, to find and embody their own inner space of love frequency through their own heart-space portal.

— —

Throughout this entire exploration, we've been referencing and holding the goal in our hearts to emit our love frequency.

But now, from a heart-based, spiritual based perspective, we can ask ourselves,

What starts to happen here, with this special occurrence that is an output and trait of all of the work that we've been doing?

Well, this is what I referenced briefly above and now underline as your emotional superpower.

I've made the point that your emotions are the bridge that connects your mind, body, and spirit,

and now this is really where your emotions coalesce and dance with your spiritual being.

Once we allow our hearts, our spirits, and the rest of our beings to emit our love frequencies, our emotions truly become our magic and our gift.

Through this realm of understanding and everything we've journeyed through thus far,

our emotions have become a communication with and a gateway back to our spiritual essences.

Let me ask you this, beautiful reader:

When we receive a spiritual download, how do we react?

When you receive intuition, when you channel, when you connect with guides, ancestors, or any of these spiritual acts, what happens in your body?

Do you have an emotional reaction?

Do you feel something?

In most cases, the answer is yes.

And I'm here to remind you that this is your power;

your emotional sensitivities through this spiritual conversation and your love frequency are the ways in which you can share more of your inner love with the outer world.

Your sensitivity and emotions are a way in which you can embody more of the spiritual being that you are with your loved ones, your friends, your family members, and the larger world.

So embrace this part of yourself.

Embrace the opening of your heart portal and the remembering of your emotional superpowers.

※

I think the most common challenge I run into with beautiful souls who come to spend time with me,

whether it's through deep meditations, activations, journeys into their spirit, or just discussing this cosmic love antenna and love frequency topic at large,

is their inability to visualize what exactly we are doing within their mind's eye.

In this chapter, in reference your heart-space portal, it's very important to understand that internal visualization is a key factor in starting to dive deeper into this portal, activating your cosmic love antenna and thus feeling your love frequency move through you.

But as stated above, most of us have trouble visualizing internally with our mind's eye.

What I'm here to propose is that you don't need to use your mind's eye for visualization.

Do not get me wrong; it can be a part of this process, and we can build that muscle, but what I am implying is that there is another visualization tool that we can use.

And this is the visualization tool of your heart.

"Heart imagery" is now an ever-growing field and understanding of consciousness within many areas of spiritual healing and science.

Put simply, your heart has the ability to share with you images that can help you dive deeper into yourself.

Just bringing your awareness and feeling sensations around your heart space can evoke this heart imagery.

We can go further by setting an intention, going into a meditation, and invoking the heart imagery of our heart-space portals with our words,

and this in itself might be enough to create and switch on the imagery of your heart.

The emphasis here is to remind you that your heart is just as powerful in its ability to help you visualize and create internal imagery for deeper awareness and healing as your mind is,

but we must be willing to allow this.

We must be willing to open this, and we must be willing to flex this muscle and allow it to show us what needs to be seen.

Let us continue now, within your powerful heart-space portal, to speak briefly on the role of manifesting within this beautiful journey that we are on.

Moving toward the internal love frequency that we ultimately wish to express in the world is not just a journey of self-discovery

but also a dynamic and a deeper relationship with manifesting more forms of love in our external world.

Whether this be through intimate partners, whether it be through loving dynamics, in our business, in our finances, in our health,

we are all wanting to manifest more forms of love. A few tips and insights to optimize this are, firstly,

releasing all expectations about and attachments to how this manifestation has to appear.

The second is acknowledging that there is no time and space within this love field that we speak of.

So the moment that you feel it in your heart and your internal world is the same moment that it becomes real.

And the third quick tip here to align with this manifesting power of your heart-space portal and your love frequency

is to understand that if you are looking to manifest a partner, as an example, and you wish to create a partner that has the characteristic of loyalty, then, being in a holographic or inter-connected universe that we exist as a part of,

a way that you can manifest and attract this loyal partner is to activate, embody, and cultivate the feeling of loyalty in yourself

because if it exists in you, then it will already exist in the partner that is attracted to your love field.

I share these quick tips on manifestation here to help you, one, open that heart-space portal a little further,

and two, give you a practical example of how your love frequency can shift your reality.

Take manifesting *action* with this love tool today.

―― ―

Let me be very clear with my words here and connect a few dots.

I've spoken about channeling numerous times throughout these chapters, including this one.

I've spoken about its connection to your cosmic love antenna and your love frequency.

All of this flows together.

But now I want to draw your attention to the connection between channeling your love antenna frequency and trauma.

Whether it be through the mental structure of your inner child, ancestral chains and your healthy ego,

whether it be through the 3D telling a story, your chakra gateways and supporting your physical pillar,

or in the spiritual, speaking about your heart-space portal and moving from the head to your mystical heart,

any trauma in these sections will add a layer of illusion onto the channel and the love frequency that wants to be emitted from you, which you innately deserve to express.

So now we can see not only the deeper role of trauma in coming back to our love frequency but also the fact that it is not there to keep us in victimhood.

It is there to be alchemized from shadow to light

so we can express ourselves and embody our love frequency to the highest potential.

If it has not been evident thus far, trauma is the treasure in the cave that you deserve to enter and open and surrender through.

9
Your Loving Divinity

t the very beginning of this beautiful book, I shared a story about my experiences as a little boy, disconnected from his sensuality, his feelings, his emotions, and something even deeper.

That something was his power, his connection to the source, the potential, and ultimately the divinity that was inside of him.

Throughout these pages, we've been taking steps through the mind, body, and now soul to ultimately synchronize these parts of our holistic being to start emitting our unique love frequency.

But the question that now bubbles up is, *Why?*

Why do we even want to express the unique frequency of our hearts and our love?

Why do we want to ignite the cosmic love antenna that we are?

Well, put very simply, it's so we can remember our divinity.

The divinity that is inside your heart portal is the frequency, and one of love.

But not just the beautiful, feminine love of receiving, of being, of allowing,

but also the masculine love of confidence, of strength, of power.

This same love frequency that, by the time you've read these words, from everything that we've talked about,

should be starting to be moving through you.

It is one of power, and that loving power is needed in this world.

Your loving divinity is supported by two very powerful energies.

This is your yin and your yang, or your feminine and your masculine.

In the physical body chapters, we spoke about yin yoga. Your yin and yang energies, or your masculine and your feminine, represent your doing and being.

When you're looking to connect to the spiritual layer of your cosmic love antenna, we must walk the line between these two energies through all of our choices and steps throughout our days, our weeks, our years, and our life.

The reason for this is that these two energies balance our inner state of being.

We cannot take inspired action on the masculine if we have not built up the energy through the feminine.

We cannot collect correct feminine-being energy if we have not allowed ourselves to first take powerful masculine action.

One cannot grow without the other, and each of these two energies can be seen in every aspect of our lives.

So if you can learn to ask yourself in any given moment, *Do I need to be more feminine in this moment?*

Or do I need to be more masculine in this moment?

You can learn to take your divine power back, for it is walking this balance that can help us express our voices,

can help us express our creation energy,

can help us express our divinity and, in the end, express our love frequency to the highest potential needed.

So where in your day today can you add more feminine?

Where in your day can you add more masculine?

Do not make this a one-off query but rather a daily muscle that you can flex and come back in to deep holistic alignment.

— —

Through the lens of your mind, in regard to your negative stories, your negative beliefs, your negative thought forms,

or your physical body trauma, pain, and dense challenges that are stored in the body itself,

all are beautiful examples of a larger disconnection from spirit and soul.

A big part of this larger story is remembering and coming back to the divine power that you've always been, despite this trauma, across your holistic being.

This is why, in various sections throughout this adventure, we've talked a lot about how emotions are the bridge between the mind and the body, the body and the spirit.

And the full synchronization at hand is because while we are not our emotions,

it is often our emotions that communicate our divinity through the mind, through the physical being, and from our heart-space portal to ultimately help us see this very fundamental truth.

— —

Most, myself included, spend so much time looking for this divine source outside of us,

whether it be in relationships, religion, or the media,

but what we can learn to come back to is finding our own unique love frequency that is the divinity that is us.

And this is really what I want to break down a little bit more for you now.

We are all unique expressions of one source; that source, for you, could be God, could be "the one mind,"

could be the quantum field, could be Buddha;

wherever and whatever you feel like this higher power is,

we are all unique expressions of this higher power.

This is something that most if not all of us can agree on.

So, if we are unique expressions of this oneness, then it must be then asserted that we contain a spark of this oneness; we contain a piece of that divinity.

Where is that piece?

What is that piece connected to?

How do we interact with and engage that piece?

Well, it is through our heart, and it is through this entire synchronization process and the enhancing of our love frequency and the activation of the cosmic love antenna that we are.

Whether it be through the mind and our beliefs,

the body and our pain and trauma release,

or the connection to our deepest spiritual practices, all of this, through the mind, body, and soul synchronization, starts to awaken and helps us to embody the divinity that we've been this entire time,

this unique expression that we are.

It is in this unique expression we are able to stand fully in our powerful love.

The love that helps us shift and change. The love that helps us transform and transmute the darkness and the love that helps us heal.

This is really what it means to be in a spiritual space of love, to emit that frequency across your mind, body, and spirit.

So as you read these words, let me ask you a question.

How does this make you feel?

How does the frequency that I'm sharing in and through these words move through your body?

How does it move through your mind?

How does it make you feel, emotionally?

Because that in itself is an answer for you.

And maybe you've felt bits and pieces of this throughout our cosmic dance, but now we're really in it.

And I'm here to tell you that what you feel is not something I am giving you.

What you feel is the divinity that is me that is speaking to the divinity that is you.

— —

Once your love frequency starts to emit and expand out from your cosmic antenna, from a spiritual view, it must be understood that your soul is constantly attracting what it needs for its highest expansion.

It is attracting from both the negative polarity and the positive polarity.

I've spoken about this prior; this is referred to as a *difficult teaching* or a *challenging teaching* or a *pain teaching*.

But if you can understand and, most important, acknowledge this, then your spiritual journey and the spiritual synchronization within your cosmic antenna will start to align itself because now you've recognized that everything is coming in for you.

Everything is attracted to your field for greater understanding and a deeper step forward.

This is a game changer for many people, and I would encourage you to open your heart to this within your loving divinity.

— —

Once your loving divinity starts to radiate through your being, and this spiritual, soulful part of you starts to synchronize with the rest of your holistic system,

something significant starts to shift, and with this comes an understanding that is very needed and appreciated in our global and collective system,

contrasted with a matrix world that thinks quite the opposite to what I am about to outline.

To go deeper, the understanding is that we are the medicine we have been looking for.

What I allude to with these words is that the more that we start to remember, feel, express, and define our internal love frequency,

the more that we also remember that we have always had the answers, the solutions and the medicine for the things that have ailed us.

We've never not had them, but what has shifted and changed is our connection to this truth.

And throughout our journey here, through the mental, physical, and spiritual realms of opening up your love frequency,

ideally, I have helped you feel and recognize just how much healing medicine you have inside of you.

You will feel the medicine that you are by being all that you are in your uniqueness and individuality.

This in itself is healing for the painful, challenging illusions in the larger global community that keep you disconnected.

—·—

Another example of how your cosmic love antenna can start to emit your divine love frequency through your soulful and spiritual realms is the act of sexual, sensual connection,

either with yourself or with a partner that you care for deeply.

What we can start to experience, and I've walked down this road myself and have had the privilege of starting to guide others to do the same,

is divinity or divine presence within the exchange of sexual pleasure.

In the previous chapter we talked about how religious trauma has disconnected us from our power and god source, and one of the ways religious trauma has exacerbated this is through the prolonged amplification of guilt and shame within the sexual act, letting many of us perceive that through our own sexual exploration, this is taking us away from God.

This is then ultimately all viewed as a sin in the eyes of religious divinity.

When you take in the larger reality, including the tantric worldview, the Vedic worldview, and many others that teach that the sacral, sensual, sexual center in conjunction with the heart-space portal,

we can now see that these are all gateways back to what your love frequency and your divinity actually is.

So the point and example that I highlight here is that if you can engage in the sexual, sensual act with the intention of connecting to your divinity or, in the case of this book, your love frequency,

then you can experience God in the sexual act itself.

And this is not something that is exclusive to me or people that I've helped.

This is a gift that we all can unwrap and unlock.

―   ―

I've noticed, on my journey and my path through this understanding of reacquainting oneself with an internal space of loving divinity, that one of the biggest challenges and pains to overcome, to move through and come back to an acceptance of power,

is the pain and the shadows that others project onto us as we awaken to our truth.

The pain and the shadows that come up with our friends, our family members, our lovers, or maybe just strangers on the internet and social media must be understood within the frame of

"hurt people hurt people."

It is much easier to project our pain onto other people than it is to go inside and surrender through, move through, and alchemize this same pain from an internal perspective.

So my advice for you here, along this path, is compassion.

Compassion for the people in pain, and compassion for yourself to move through this.

We cannot fight fire with fire, but we can fight fire with love.

So use this *divine* reminder here in this moment.

As we get to the end of this journey of activating your cosmic love antenna and your beautiful love frequency, in this chapter, which explains your divinity and the truth of what you are, I want to bring your attention to the power of holding space for another.

And what I mean by this is much more than holding the therapeutic space for another, much like a coach, a therapist, a doctor, or a counsellor.

While this is powerful and beautiful, what I'm implying here is about holding space for another, tapped into the loving divinity and love frequency that you are now starting to emit.

When you hold space for another spiritual being having a human experience, when you hold space connected to your love frequency and the divinity that's inside of you,

something very special happens.

Something inside of you connects to something inside of that person.

When you allow the fullest expression of your love frequency and thus your inner divinity to permeate the space you create for another,

this awakens their essence, and whether they are consciously aware of it or not,

what you are doing is allowing them to feel and acknowledge their light.

What you're allowing the other person in the space to do is to remember what they are.

We've all experienced this when listening to someone that we resonate with.

When you tune into a motivational speaker, let's say, using the example of Tony Robbins, do you connect only to what he is logically saying, or do you also feel, through your mind, body, and spirit, something much more?

Do you feel a resonance?

Do you feel a power?

Do you feel a recognition?

I would assert that this is your love frequency that is being seen in the space that this person is creating, and it is waking up.

This is something we can all do for each other, and I will come back to this at the end of our journey.

An example I want to share here, within all of this conversation and discussion around your loving godliness,

is that once we start to accept our divine nature, and start emitting our love frequency because of this, it doesn't just come with a lot of affirmation and reassurance of the power we've been the whole time;

it also comes with a remembering of the beautiful gifts we are here to share with the world.

And this is significant because with some of the work that I've done with past lives and regressions and deep meditative journeys into individuals' soul lines,

what I can say with a large degree of certainty is that there are many souls, maybe even in you, reading these words right now,

that are coming into this current incarnation with a lot of, let's say, history behind them.

These souls are here not just to be healers working on their own, but to specifically help transition all of us into this collective awakening that we've all seen, to a degree, over the last few years.

And while this, like many of the themes discussed prior, could be a whole conversation in itself,

I share this in this chapter to encourage the beautiful being that you are, and this is a part of the larger conversation, activation

and the ignition of the truth and the divine responsibility that you're here to embrace.

An understanding must now be illuminated once more around what healing and pain are through this divine spiritual lens.

What I mean by this is, let's just take out the single word that is *pain*.

For a lot of you, reading this word probably comes with a lot of baggage, resistance, and suppression still at this point in our adventure together.

I'm right there with you.

But what if we flip this on its head one more time?

What if, instead of pain being something we looked away from, pain came with the understanding that has rippled through this book:

a beautiful communicator of what needs to be seen, what needs to be addressed, what needs to be delved into.

This is something we have discussed from a few different angles.

Now let's take this term that is *soul fragment*.

And let's mash this together with the role of pain healing not just across the spiritual realm but the physical, mental, and emotional as well.

When we combine pain, soul fragments, and the healing journey, something very interesting takes place. We remember that we never needed to gain anything through our pain and our healing journey.

What we needed to do was pause, take a moment and lovingly attach each soul fragment back into the hole.

What is a soul fragment?

A soul fragment is a piece of our being,

be it spiritual, mental, emotional, or physical, that is detached from the whole—not detached as in lost forever

but still attached in stasis, giving us triggers and communication.

So, how can we come back to our wholeness?

What are these triggers?

These are the communications that the pain is giving us to lead us to deeper awareness around the fragments themselves.

So you're starting to see the bigger picture here. When we can see all of this in one big unit, the outcome of this healing of the pain signals and corresponding soul fragment union

is not just our loving divinity but this frequency of love we wish to emit.

One last time here now we must hold space and discuss a further challenge around the acceptance of our loving divinity and the shadows of religious trauma.

I'll only speak from my own journey and tell you

that whether it be self-sacrifice, a fear of death and hell, god keeping score, a suppression of my sexuality, sensuality, and sexual desires (as discussed earlier), or even the deep-seated feelings of unworthiness and not being good enough—

many different components that lead to the same outcome of fearing and pushing away this idea that we are divine and powerful beings—

that we are godly beings, that we have the divine presence and source within us.

So my love goes to you if you read these words, and you are still triggered and traumatized by them.

But I also acknowledge that this love can help you move through this kind of trauma.

If I can move through these wounds, then you can also, and if we're looking to embody our love frequency, it is these very wounds that can be alchemized back into our truth.

So I encourage you to go deeper into these pains.

Because I can assure you that there is a light at the end of this tunnel, and a big part and example of this is the letter of love you're reading now.

— —

A final practice, tool, and concept to help you grasp your loving divinity from another view

is a series of deep dives into your psyche that I often help clients go deeper into,

and that is the practice of lucid dreaming.

In this novel thus far, I've referred to dreaming a couple of times.

But now, in this chapter, I wish to explain to you the practice of lucid dreaming to emphasize just how powerful you, as the individual, actually are.

For those new to lucid dreaming, put simply, it is the art of becoming self-aware within your dreams at night.

This is the analogy I like to use to explain this, which most practitioners of this art will know some version of:

Imagine you are a passenger on an airplane moving across a vast sky.

You, as the passenger on the plane, are the flow of the dream itself, and the sky and its elements are the creator or the essence of the dream.

Now, when you're having a normal dream, you are the passenger in the plane moving through the sky and weather;

you have no control.

You're just observing what occurs.

When you become lucid, however,

you become the pilot or the captain that directs the movement of the dream but does not control the dream essence itself.

Now, what does this have to do with your divinity and your love frequency?

Once you start to obtain lucidity in the dreamscape (through various methods such as journaling, affirmations and devotion),

you start to realize just how powerful you are,

you start to realize just how wonderful and magical your essence is through what you can create in your dream world.

As just one beautiful example of this,

we can actually learn, in our lucid state in the dreams, to meditate!

And as many teachers have described, meditating in the dreamscape is taking the practice to a mastery level because, put very simply, you are breaking through extra layers of illusion and consciousness.

I share this practice to help your brain and, most important, your heart understand and conceptualize just what you're capable of,

and if you start anything today, please make it pursuing an understanding and an acceptance of your divine power, not just through your dreams

but through your life in general.

―

With all of the talk of divinity, God, and your internal power in this chapter, it's a surprise that it's taken me this long to mention the term *ascension*.

Ascension is probably one of the most popular and highly debated terms within the spiritual community.

And I wish to add it in now, as we tie up this spirit and soul part of your synchronization and this larger cosmic love antenna and love frequency journey,

because there is something very significant that most of us are not acknowledging around the ascension process, and understanding this can empower you to take all of these teachings and embody them in your 3D world.

When you start to emit your beautiful, unique frequency of love, you are not admitting it as an individual that is disconnected.

You are emitting it as an interconnected part of an ever-evolving, ever-ascending, loving collective.

You are a unique, loving soul expression of one source. That source, for you, could be God, could be the divine, could be the quantum field, wherever you land.

You lovingly refer to this one source as the space from which all of our soul expressions extend.

So, with that understanding, we can now go back to this idea of ascension and see that ascension is not an individual thing.

We can only ascend if we ascend together.

With this view, we can now apply the understanding that if I, Harrison, or you, the beautiful reader, start to emit your beautiful frequency of love,

by doing this act, we are adding into the collective. Not just adding into the collective as a random act but adding to the love frequency of the collective overall so it can ascend.

So you doing all of this work is adding to the evolution of us as a species.

And this is what it truly means to ascend.

We ascend through the group, and we ascend through loving expression of *all* that we truly are meant to be.

That is Love.

Conclusion

As we conclude this beautiful love journey together, I want to point out two very mystical and profound understandings.

This path that we have taken and all the steps along the way

have hopefully opened your love frequency, and it is now flowing powerfully and abundantly up your cosmic love antenna and out into the world.

If you're now noticing this, experiencing this, and feeling this

(if not, it is only a matter of time, based on your consciousness expansion and all that you have remembered in this book),

you have also gained a very important ability, and that ability is to be a distortion-free,

trauma-free,

pain-free mirror of love for someone else.

For when we are free, we are not denying the shadow's inevitable return, but we are saying that we will love ourselves through it and not be taken away by it.

So acknowledge today that the more work we do on ourselves,

the more our light and our love start to expand.

Throughout this journey, you have seen this as you've been exploring the different parts of your cosmic love antenna and all that inhibits your love frequency from flowing.

All of this is accessible to each and every one of us, and when you stand in the pillar of love that you are,

you become this mirror for other lost souls.

This is your power, and this is a gift that you can now embrace, a gift I've given you in these pages and a gift I encourage you to share with all that you love.

Finally, we live in a world where it is very easy for us to look externally for the voice, the authority, and the power to help us take a step forward.

Throughout these pages, my hope and intention has also been to awaken that same power inside of you.

When we open and activate our love frequency through our cosmic love antenna, through mind, body, and soul synchronization, a side effect is the activation and strengthening of your own internal voice.

This internal voice has been there from the beginning, despite your pains, despite the inner-child trauma, the ancestral chains, the 3D telling a story, the physical limitations, or the spiritual disconnection.

What has been different and shifted is our ability, as individuals, to listen,

and our ability to create our own internal space, to hold ourselves, to allow the energy of this voice to flow through us across mind, body, and spirit.

So my final desire as I write this conclusion is that this love frequency is not just moving through but that it is also reminding you of this voice

and this knowledge, which you can always turn back to.

This voice and knowledge is there when your body feels sick.

This voice and knowledge is there when you're looking to bring about a new relationship in your life.

This voice and knowledge is there when you feel scared and unsafe.

And this voice and knowledge is there when you're looking for deeper layers of mystical, spiritual awakening.

So take action today to allow this voice to speak.

Remember to ask the questions that need to be answered and to surrender through fear with confidence, courage, and spiritual love

so that this voice is your main authority and is never quiet again.

Love you.

Resources

If you desire extra loving support, guidance, or just education on any of the tools, concepts, or themes within this book, I would refer you to the following bonus spiritual *love* resources:

The *Cosmic Love Antenna* Podcast (available on Apple, Spotify, Google, and all main platforms)

One-on-one Cosmic Love Antenna Coaching and Mentoring with Harrison (www.harrisonmeagher.com/learn-more – SUBSCRIBE for updates, news and freebies)

@harrisonmeagher on all social platforms (Instagram, Facebook, LinkedIn, TikTok, YouTube)